International Relations Theory

'... offers something that has been missing from the critical IR literature ever since its initial formulations over a decade ago: a breakthrough textbook that will allow a much wider audience of undergraduate students to understand how – and, more importantly, *why* – critical IR asks the sort of questions it does.'

Peter Mandaville, *University of Kent*

International Relations Theory: a critical introduction is an innovative new textbook, which introduces students to the main theories in international relations. Written by an experienced teacher of the subject, it also analyses each theory allowing students not only to understand them, but also to critically engage with the assumptions and myths that underpin them. It does this by using five familiar films as tools for first understanding each theory and then for understanding the myths that make them so persuasive for some people.

Key features of this textbook include:

- Coverage of the main theories and traditions including: realism and neorealism; idealism and neoidealism; liberalism; constructivism; postmodernism; gender; globalization and the 'end of history'.
- Innovative use of narratives from five famous films that students will be familiar with: *Lord of the Flies*; *Independence Day*; *Wag the Dog*; *Fatal Attraction*; and *The Truman Show*.
- An accessible writing style, providing students with boxed key concepts, guides to further reading and thinking.

This breakthrough textbook has been designed to unravel the complexities of international relations theory in a way that allows students a clearer idea of how the theories work, and some of the myths that are associated with them.

Cynthia Weber is Professor of International Studies at the University of Leeds. She has previously taught at Purdue University and has held visiting appointments at the University of Southern California, University of Wales, Aberystwyth, and The Queen's University, Belfast.

International Relations Theory

■ A critical introduction

Cynthia Weber

Routledge
Taylor & Francis Group

LONDON AND NEW YORK

First published 2001
by Routledge
11 New Fetter Lane, London EC4P 4EE

Simultaneously published in the USA and
Canada
by Routledge
29 West 35th Street, New York, NY 10001

Reprinted 2003

*Routledge is an imprint of the Taylor & Francis
Group*

© 2001 Cynthia Weber

Typeset in Century Old Style by Keystroke,
Jacaranda Lodge, Wolverhampton
Printed and bound in Great Britain by
TJ International Ltd, Padstow, Cornwall

British Library Cataloguing in Publication Data
A catalogue record for this book is available
from the British Library

*Library of Congress Cataloguing in Publication
Data*
Weber, Cynthia
   International relations theory: a critical
   introduction / Cynthia Weber.
   p. cm.
   Includes bibliographical references and
   index.
   1. International relations. I. Title.
   JZ1305 .W43 2001
   327.1′01—dc21   00–068432

ISBN 0–415–24973–2 (hbk)
ISBN 0–415–24974–0 (pbk)

For Lyn and Charles Weber

and

for Bob DiClerico

Learning depends upon freeing the message from the constraints of the situation at hand

Roland Barthes

Contents

Plates

Figures

Tables

Boxes

Note to teachers

After a sabbatical from Purdue University a few years ago, I couldn't wait to get back into the classroom. I had missed my interactions with students and had a renewed appreciation for the practice of teaching. But I had a number of problems. Like many teachers, I had intellectually outgrown my well-worn way of introducing international politics and international relations (IR) theory to students, but I never had the time to do more than tinker with examples or simulation exercises in an attempt to remedy this. Also, as at many other universities, the introductory course I taught in international relations was a prerequisite for later courses. As such, it was expected to familiarize students with key themes from long-standing IR traditions like realism, idealism, historical materialism, and their neo's, and introduce them to new perspectives like constructivism, postmodernism, gender, and globalization. This could be done by opting for an approach that narrated the historical development of IR traditions and debates or, alternatively, for a more topical approach to the subject and the field. Beyond these two standard options, there were no others.

My experiments in the classroom with these teaching techniques left me feeling both fulfilled and disappointed. I was pretty good at narrating the traditions of IR theory, situating them historically, and bringing them into lively conversation with one another. This allowed me to explore some exciting topics in the field as well, which students seemed to enjoy. All this was fulfilling. But I was disappointed with how students interacted with IR theory. Despite my best critical intentions, students would find a particular aspect of IR theory they could identify with, attach themselves to it as 'the way things are', and evaluate every other IR theory they would hear in relation to it. Most often, this theory was realism. Occasionally, it was idealism. And in some cases, it was historical materialism or gender. It wasn't that I cared which theory students attached themselves to. I didn't prefer them to believe one theory over another. My aim was to get them to critically rethink *all* the theories. And I failed miserably.

Why did I fail? If a theory is presented to students as if it narrates just the way things are in international politics and if this way of making sense of the world taps into students' own preconceptions about the world, then it is extremely difficult to get them to think critically about the theory. So I had to do better. But how? How could I both stick to the brief of what an introduction to international relations or IR theory is generally supposed to be and at the same time present the IR theories and topics in ways that allow for their genuine critical reconsideration?

International Relations Theory: A Critical Introduction is my answer to this question. Its approach is both traditional and non-traditional. It is traditional because it is organized around the major traditions of international relations theory – realism, idealism, historical materialism, constructivism, gender, and globalization. It is non-traditional because it reexamines these IR traditions by asking the critical question, what makes the stories these IR traditions tell about international politics *appear* to be true? What, for example, makes realism's story about sovereign nation-states locked into a battle for survival or idealism's story about the possibilities of international cooperation so compelling? In this book I suggest that what makes these IR stories appear to be true are the IR myths upon which they are based.

IR myths are *apparent truths*, usually expressed as slogans, that IR traditions rely upon in order to appear to be true. The 'truth' or the 'falsity' of an IR myth is beside the point. Examining how an IR myth functions to make an IR tradition appear to be true is the point. So, for example, the IR myth 'international anarchy is the permissive cause of war' is the *apparent truth* that realism and these days neorealism depend upon. Similarly, 'there is an international society' is the IR myth that makes the stories told by idealism and neoidealism appear to be true.

None of this should come as a surprise to IR theorists. We know that different IR traditions rely upon very different IR myths in order to appear to be true. So how do we make sense of these contradictory ways of seeing the world for our students? The usual strategy is to 'test' the validity of the IR myths against the 'facts' of international politics to determine which IR myth (and therefore which IR tradition) offers the most accurate description of international politics. Proving that an IR myth, tradition, or theory is wrong so that it can be replaced by another one which is 'true' is usually what we mean by doing 'critical IR theory'.

But what if we push our analysis just a bit further? What if we unpack not just IR traditions but the IR myths upon which they are based? What if we ask of IR myths (as we do of IR traditions), what makes the story they tell about international politics appear to be true? What makes international anarchy *appear* to be the permissive cause of war, or why does there *appear* to be an international society?

If we pursue these questions, then we not only push our analysis of IR traditions further. We push what it means to do 'critical IR theory'. Why is this the case? Because the alternative way of doing critical IR theory proposed in this book allows us to examine not only how one 'truth' replaces another 'truth' but also how 'truths' get constructed. This is beyond the scope of most traditional critical IR theory which concerns itself only with evaluating which 'truth' appears to be most 'true'. By declaring one theory 'true' and another one 'false', traditional critical IR theory cannot then go back and examine what makes the 'true' theory *appear* to be true. For example, realism critiques idealism by 'proving' that its IR myth, 'international anarchy is the permissive cause of war', is 'more true' than idealism's myth, 'there is an international society'. But, in so doing, realism cannot ask what makes its IR myth about international anarchy *appear* to be true. And, without critically analysing its own IR myth, realism ultimately proves nothing.

Asserting the 'truth' of one IR myth over another in no way guarantees the 'truth' of an IR myth, no matter how much empirical evidence is amassed to support the 'truth' of the myth. This is the case because the 'truth' of an IR myth depends as much upon *how* empirical evidence is organized into a coherent story about international politics as it does on the evidence alone. This is a central problem with how critical theory is usually practised in the discipline of international relations.

International Relations Theory takes this problem seriously. How it takes it seriously is by shifting its analytical emphasis away from looking for 'empirical evidence' to support the 'truth' of an IR myth towards an investigation of the *organization* of the 'facts' that make an IR story about international politics *appear* to be true. Doing critical IR theory in this way means we have to suspend our usual preoccupation with getting to the 'real truth' about an IR myth, tradition, or theory and ask instead, what makes a particular story about international politics *appear to be true*? Or, to put it somewhat differently, how does the 'truth' function in a particular IR myth?

It is not accidental that this book as my answer to how to teach IR theory better should focus on stories and how they are told. If the world is made up of 'facts' and stories that organize those 'facts', then there is no more important skill to pass on to students than to make them better readers and writers of stories, better interpreters of not just the 'facts' but of the organization of the 'facts'. With this in mind, *International Relations Theory* does not try to be a comprehensive textbook crammed with every 'fact' about international life or even international theory. By focusing on the major IR traditions of realism, idealism, historical materialism, constructivism, postmodernism, gender, and globalization, it attempts to help students to read and write their world better by arming them with the ability to critically ask, how does the 'truth' get told?

Hopefully, all this takes me far along the critical road to teaching IR theory. But it leaves me with one more major problem. How do I get students interested in doing alternative critical IR theory? What could possibly motivate and engage students who are so often bored with reading and writing and who are likely to find IR theory incomprehensible at first?

Good teaching means starting where your students are and bringing them to where you want them to be, rather than always expecting them to know how to come to where you are. Over the years, I have found that students enjoy engaging with visual media. Students are into television and film. And, what's more, they tend to be excellent readers and writers of visual media. To get students to be better readers and writers of IR theory, the place to start is to get them to apply what they already know about reading and writing visual media to international politics.

How do I do this? By teaching them IR theory through popular films that they know about and like. That's why this book uses *Lord of the Flies* to teach students about how the anarchy myth works in realism and neorealism, *Independence Day* to teach them about how the international society myth functions in idealism and neoidealism, *Wag the Dog* to introduce them to the debates around social constructivism and postmodernism, *Fatal Attraction* to make them aware of the political stakes of thinking about gender as a variable, and *The Truman Show* to reconsider the myth that history is over and how this myth supports neoliberal stories about 'globalization'.

As this brief synopsis illustrates, I use popular films as vehicles through which students can rethink IR theory and IR myths. The films are used not only to illustrate a particular IR myth but to show students something more besides, and this something more is how the IR myth functions. Put differently, popular films not only illustrate IR myths and the IR traditions they support. Popular films provide students with answers to the question, how does an IR myth *appear* to be true? In so doing, popular films point to how politics, power, and ideology are culturally constructed and how the culture of IR theory might be politically reconstructed.

Again, this should not surprise IR theorists, especially those who are attentive to the current debates concerning IR theory and popular culture. For my starting point is to think about IR theory as a site of cultural practice, and this book is a critical reconsideration of what must go without saying in order for the traditional cultural practices of IR theory to function.

It is written with undergraduate students in English-speaking universities in mind. It can be used on its own to structure an introductory course on international relations or IR theory, or it can be used to supplement either historical/theoretical or topical presentations of IR. Each myth is accompanied by 'Suggestions for further thinking'. These suggestions make the book adaptable to lecture- or seminar-style teaching and extend and upgrade the material from the undergraduate level to the graduate level.

It was also written with my colleagues in mind. I hope it will offer them insights about innovative ways of teaching as well as about the disciplinary culture of IR theory.

I have many people to thank for their intellectual generosity towards me and this project. The sage advice of Jim Rosenau, who encouraged me as I prepared for my first teaching post to combine my teaching and my research by being theoretically imaginative in the classroom, and of Cynthia Enloe, whose challenge to us all to write accessibly and for a general readership, oriented me as I undertook this project. At Purdue University, I benefited enormously from conversations with colleagues, including Bob Bartlett, Pat Boling, Berenice Carroll, Ann Clark, Rosie Clawson, Keith Shimko, Mark Tilton, Michael Weinstein, Linda White, and Lee Wilson. While I may not have discussed this project directly with some of these colleagues, they contributed to the project nonetheless by providing a supportive intellectual environment and a place for me to experiment with my teaching. Graduate students in my 'IR Myths' course, especially Julie Webber, Deems Morrione, and Maartin Rothman, and undergraduate students in 'Alternative IR', provided invaluable insights for this project.

Moving to the United Kingdom in 1999 meant that I gained a number of new critical eyes on the project. At the University of Leeds, Kevin Theakston granted me a timely sabbatical which allowed me to finish the book. Other colleagues in the Institute of Politics and International Studies, especially Hugh Dyer, Jason Ralph, and Rhiannon Vickers, and in the Institute for Communication Studies, especially Jayne Rodgers, were particularly supportive. My students in my undergraduate course 'Popular Culture and International Relations' at the University of Leeds acted as my final sounding board for the manuscript before its publication. They saved me from many a misstep.

The invitation from Bob Eccleshall of the School of Politics at The Queen's University of Belfast to spend my sabbatical in the School allowed me to finish the manuscript there and to receive helpful feedback on the project from students and colleagues at Queen's, especially Alan Finlayson. I also benefited from presenting some of this material at the University of Kent London Centre for International Relations, where I particularly would like to thank Vivienne Jabri and Jef Huysmans for their detailed comments.

Yale Furguson and Barry Jones provided me with my first forum in which to experiment with the mixing of film and international theory – on the New Frontiers panel at the 1998 European Consortium for Political Research meetings in Vienna. Taking a chance on this unusual form, Walter Carlsnaes published the resulting paper as 'IR: The Resurrection OR New Frontiers of Incorporation' in the *European Journal of International Relations*, 5(4): 435–50 (1999), which forms the basis for arguments presented in Chapters 4 and 5.

My editor at Routledge, Mark Kavanagh, offered support and advice throughout. His belief in and enthusiasm for this project was much appreciated. Mark's advice, and the thoughtful reviews of this manuscript by Roxanne Doty and by two anonymous referees, made this a better text.

François Debrix read the entire manuscript, commenting on it as I produced it. He is a wonderful reader and writer of stories, and I thank him for his intellectual generosity. If it hadn't been for Marysia Zalewski, who encouraged me to tell my stories about IR theory using film and who forced me to consider the bigger intellectual and political picture at every turn, this book could not have been written. Nor could this book have been written without the intellectual guidance of John MacLean, Richard Ashley, Thaïs Morgan, and Diane Rubenstein, each of whom introduced me to a different mode of critical thinking. I thank them all.

This book is dedicated to my folks, Lyn and Charles Weber, whose support and encouragement especially over these past few years has been invaluable. This book is also dedicated to Bob DiClerico, a professor at West Virginia University, where I studied as an undergraduate. It was his great skill as a teacher that encouraged my own enthusiasm for teaching. It is his example of excellence that guides my teaching to this day.

The authors and publishers would like to thank the following for granting permission to reproduce material in this work.

Dialogue quoted from the following films are transcripts made by the author:

Lord of the Flies (1963), directed by Peter Brook, based on the novel by William Golding.

Independence Day (1996), directed by Roland Emmerich, screenplay by Dean Devlin and Roland Emmerich.

Wag the Dog (1997), directed by Barry Levinson, screenplay by Hilary Henkin and David Mamet.

Fatal Attraction (1987), directed by Adrian Lyne, screenplay by James Dearden.

The Truman Show (1998), directed by Peter Weir, screenplay by Andrew Niccol.

Every effort has been made to contact copyright holders for their permission to reprint material in this book. The publishers would be grateful to hear from any copyright holder who is not here acknowledged and will undertake to rectify any errors or omissions in future editions of this book.

Chapter 1

Introduction

Culture, ideology, and the myth function in IR theory

International politics is a huge field. It explores everything from wars to revolutions to global gender inequalities to demands for international human rights to international trade. To try to make sense of international politics, we often turn to international relations theory. IR theory makes organizing generalizations about international politics. IR theory is a collection of stories about the world of international politics. And in telling stories about international politics, IR theory doesn't just present what is going on in the world out there. IR theory also imposes its own vision of what the world out there looks like.

We use IR theory to make sense of the world of international politics. But how do we make sense of IR theory? Of course, we can learn all the stories IR theory tells us about the world. We call these stories IR traditions and name them (neo)realism, (neo)idealism, historical materialism, constructivism, gender, and globalization. But just learning the stories IR theory tells doesn't tell us much about IR theory itself. It doesn't tell us, for example, how IR theory works. What makes the stories IR theory tells about international politics so compelling? What makes the stories IR theory tells about the world of international politics *appear to be true*?

My answer is that IR theory – a collection of stories about international politics – relies upon IR myths in order to appear to be true. What is an IR myth? An IR myth is an *apparent truth*, usually expressed in slogan form, that an IR theory relies upon in order to *appear to be true*. IR myths, in other words, are the building blocks of IR theory, of the stories IR theory tells about the world of international politics. They are that part of the story that is so familiar to us that we take it for granted. And our taking IR myths for granted is necessary for IR theories to appear to be true.

For example, think of the slogans 'international anarchy is the permissive cause of war' and 'there is an international society'. Such slogans are IR myths. Realists rely upon the knowledge that 'international anarchy is the permissive cause of war' to explain why sovereign nation-states inevitably find themselves in conflict with one another and why balance of power politics is the key to managing such conflict. Idealists, in contrast, rely upon the knowledge that 'there is an international society' in order for them to be able to tell their stories about progress among sovereign nation-states on a global scale to the point that conflict among them might be transcended. If we questioned these IR myths, then the stories told by IR traditions like realism and idealism would not necessarily appear to be true.

Why do I refer to these building blocks of IR theory as IR myths? Is it because I believe IR myths – like myths generally – are false? Absolutely not! IR myths may be true, and they may be false. The truth or falsity of an IR myth is not important for understanding how IR myths function as the building blocks of IR theory. So why call the building blocks of IR stories IR myths? I call them IR myths because of the 'mythologizing function' or 'myth function' they perform. It is the myth function of these building blocks of IR theory that makes the stories told by IR theory appear to be true.

What is the myth function in IR theory? How do IR myths make an IR theory appear to be true? And why is it important for us to study the process by which IR myths make IR theories appear to be true?

These are the questions I address in this chapter. I do so by considering IR theory's relationship to three concepts – culture, ideology, and the myth function.

Culture

Raymond Williams, a pioneer in the field of cultural studies and cultural theory, noted of the term culture that it is 'one of the two or three most complicated words in the English language' (Williams, 1983:87). Williams has a point. Culture is one of those terms that everyone seems to understand but no one seems to be able to define adequately.

Often, when we think of culture, we think of traditional arrangements within particular states or societies. For example, we may say that there is something called US culture or UK culture. But this way of thinking about culture suggests that there is something stable, identifiable, and generalizable that we can point to as a culture. When we unpack a term like 'US culture', we find so many contradictions, incompatibilities, and complexities within it that the term itself seems to mean little. For example, how can we meaningfully make sense of the militia movement, the religious right, rugged individualism, and anti-capitalism, not to mention regional, rural, class, race, sexuality, and age 'sub-cultures' collected under the one term 'US culture'? Not very easily.

For this reason, theorists who think about what culture is have tried to come up with less static and more open definitions of culture. These definitions focus on how culture is related to meaning rather than try to pin culture to a particular place at a particular time, like the contemporary US (see Box 1.1). According to Stuart Hall, this is because 'culture . . . is not so much a set of *things* – novels and paintings or TV programmes and comics – as a process, a set of *practices*', what others have called 'signifying practices' (Hall, 1997:2; Storey, 1997:2). For Hall, 'culture is concerned with the production and the exchange of meanings – the "giving and taking of meaning" – between members of a society or group' (1997:2). Or, as John Hartley defines it, culture is 'The social production and reproduction of sense, meaning, and consciousness' (1994:68). Culture has to do with how we make sense of the world and how we produce, reproduce, and circulate that sense.

We circulate our sense about the world in many ways, and one of these ways is through stories. This is why another cultural theorist, Clifford Geertz, described culture as 'an ensemble of stories we tell about ourselves' (Geertz, 1975:448). For Geertz, these stories are not always conscious. They can be composed of beliefs we consciously hold as well as of habits we unconsciously perform. Cultural stories are

---

Box 1.1 What is culture?

'culture is concerned with the production and the exchange of meanings – the "giving and taking of meaning" – between members of a society or group' (Hall, 1997)

'The social production and reproduction of sense, meaning, and consciousness' (John Hartley, in O'Sullivan et al., 1994)

'an ensemble of stories we tell about ourselves' (Geertz, 1975)

composed of both sense (consciousness) and common sense (unconsciousness). Common sense is what we know but don't think about, what Roland Barthes described as 'what-goes-without-saying' (Barthes, 1972:11).

Studying culture understood as 'sense making', 'signifying practices', or 'an ensemble of stories, beliefs, and habits' means we have to pay attention to how meanings are made. We must think about how meaning-making relies upon what is said and what goes without saying. And we must recognize that cultures aren't just 'there', fully formed for us to study. Indeed, it may be impossible for us to identify 'cultures' as objects of study at all. Studying culture means looking at how what we objectify as 'culture' is made. And part of what makes culture and helps to distinguish some 'cultures' from other 'cultures' are cultural practices that produce, organize, and circulate meanings through stories told about the world.

IR theory can be studied as a site of cultural practice. IR theory is 'an ensemble of stories' told about the world it studies, which is the world of international politics. Studying IR theory as a site of cultural practice means being attentive to how IR theory makes sense of the world of international politics. We have to ask of IR theory: how do the stories it tells about the world of international politics become sense and common sense? And why do we take for granted the sense IR theory makes of our lives in relation to international politics?

My answer to these questions is that IR theory relies upon IR myths in order to transform its culturally produced stories about the world into common sense about the world that we take for granted. But before we explore this process in detail, let me introduce another important concept that plays a part in this process. This concept is ideology.

Ideology

Unlike the term culture, ideology is a term for which formal definitions abound (see Box 1.2). The way ideology is most commonly defined is as 'a fairly coherent and comprehensive set of ideas that explains and evaluates social conditions, helps people understand their place in society, and provides a program for social and political action' (Ball and Dagger, 1995:9). It is a ready-made set of meanings and interpretations that can help us to make sense of our world and tell us how to act in relation to it.

This way of defining ideology assumes that all ideologies are consciously held. And many are. Examples of 'conscious ideologies' are liberalism, conservatism, socialism, feminism, ecologism, and even vegetarianism. Conscious ideologies are easily identifiable. We know what they are, and we can subscribe to them or reject them.

While conscious ideologies like liberalism and conservatism are powerful because they can politically mobilize people and 'raise consciousness' about political situations, another type of ideologies – 'unconscious ideologies' – are arguably even more politically powerful. Unlike neatly packaged, easily identifiable, named ideologies, unconscious ideologies lack proper names. This makes us less likely to be able to identify them as ideologies. This is why they are also called 'anonymous ideologies' (Barthes, 1972).

Box 1.2 What is ideology?

Conscious ideology: 'a fairly coherent and comprehensive set of ideas that explains
    and evaluates social conditions, helps people understand their place in society,
    and provides a program for social and political action' (Ball and Dagger,
    1995)

Unconscious ideology: ideology that is not formally named and that is therefore
    difficult to identify. It is the common-sense foundation of our worldviews that is
    beyond debate.

An example of an unconscious ideology is 'boys will be boys'. It would be
difficult to attribute this ideology to anyone in particular both because no one person
or one ideological tradition claims it as their own and because it appears to those
who hold it to be 'just the way things are' or the way things ought to be. In this sense,
unconscious ideologies are 'profoundly unconscious' (Althusser, 1969). We use them
to help us make sense of our worlds, very often without realizing it. And because we
don't realize we hold unconscious ideologies or use them to make sense of our
worlds, we very rarely interrogate them. We very rarely ask difficult questions about
them that might upset them as common sense (see Box 1.3).

If conscious ideologies are those ideologies packaged as programmes for
political action that we debate in the political arena, unconscious ideologies are the
foundations of our ideological and political thinking that we place beyond debate.
Unconscious ideologies, in other words, 'go without saying'. We don't like to have our
unconscious ideologies – our common sense – articulated, much less questioned.
When they are, our way of making sense of the world is potentially threatened.

How is ideology related to culture? If culture is a site of meaning production,
ideology is a site where meanings that are culturally produced are transformed into
just the way things are or the way things ought to be. Some of this is done explicitly.
For example, if you declare your allegiance to a particular named conscious ideology
like conservatism, you are declaring that conservatism truly describes how the world
is and how it ought to be. You are consciously transforming your cultural views about
the world into *the* view of the world as it naturally is.

Box 1.3 Examples of conscious and unconscious ideologies

Conscious ideologies	*Unconscious ideologies*
Liberalism	Boys will be boys
Conservatism	America has a classless society
Socialism	English people are white
Feminism	Everyone I know is straight

But a lot of the transformation from the cultural to the ideological goes without saying because it employs anonymous, unconscious ideologies. In this respect, unconscious ideologies are akin to cultural habits. We enact them all the time without thinking about them. And, in the case of unconscious ideologies, these unconscious habits in our thinking transform what is cultural or produced into what appears to be natural or just the way things are (Barthes, 1972).

It is this process of transforming meanings from cultural to natural that I want to explore in relation to IR theory and IR myths. And it is this process that is explained though the myth function in IR theory.

The myth function

IR theory is a site of cultural practice in which conscious and unconscious ideologies are circulated through stories that *appear* to be true. The stories we recognize and hold consciously we call IR traditions (like realism and idealism). The stories we don't recognize as ideologies because we don't have names for them and hold unconsciously I call IR myths (like 'international anarchy is the permissive cause of war' and 'there is an international society') (see Box 1.4).

While we debate the 'truth' of IR stories organized into IR tradition, we rarely reflect on why these stories seem to make so much sense. In other words, we rarely consider how unconscious ideologies or IR myths function in these stories called IR traditions. Rather, we generally accept IR myths as forthright expressions of how the world works, and we allow these IR myths to function as the building blocks of IR traditions that narrate complicated explanations of how the world is and how it ought to be (see Box 1.5).

If IR theory narrates a particular view of the world from the perspective of various IR traditions, an IR myth is what helps make a particular view of the world *appear* to be true. The *myth function* in IR theory is the transformation of what is particular, cultural, and ideological (like a story told by an IR tradition) into what *appears* to be universal, natural, and purely empirical. It is naturalizing meanings – making them into common sense – that are the products of cultural practices (Barthes, 1972). Put another way, the myth function in IR theory is making a 'fact' out of an interpretation.

Why describe this process as the myth function in IR theory? Because this process of making what is cultural and disputed into what is natural and therefore goes without saying is the work or the function IR myths perform in IR theory.

Box 1.4 What is an IR myth?

An IR myth is an *apparent truth*, usually expressed as a slogan, that an IR theory or tradition (like realism or idealism) relies upon in order to appear to be true.

Examples: 'international anarchy is the permissive cause of war'; and 'there is an international society'.

> **Box 1.5 What is the myth function in IR theory?**
>
> The *myth function* in IR theory is the transformation of what is particular, cultural, and ideological (like a story told by an IR tradition) into what *appears* to be universal, natural, and purely empirical
>
> Cultural interpretation → Myth function → 'Natural fact'

Analysing how these transformations from cultural meanings into naturalized facts occur in our everyday encounters with IR theory is the purpose of this book. And by undertaking this analysis, we are not only examining the intersections of IR theory and everyday cultural practices. We are also analysing the intersections of IR theory and political power. Why is this the case?

Transforming the cultural into the natural is a highly political practice that depends upon all sorts of complex configurations of power. Precisely how power works to mythologize something cultural into something natural varies from context to context. But in a general sense, *power works through myths by appearing to take the political out of the ideological*. This is because something that appears to be natural and unalterable also appears to be apolitical. Yet these sorts of 'natural facts' are arguably the most intensely political stories of all, not just because of what they say (what the specific myth is) but because of what they do (they remove themselves and the tradition they support from political debate). This is why Barthes refers to myths as 'depoliticized speech' (Barthes, 1972).

'Re-politicizing' IR theory and IR myths requires us to suspend our interest in the 'truth' of IR theory (whether or not a specific theoretical interpretation is really right or wrong) so we can refocus our attention on how cultural configurations of power and ideology make a theory or story *appear* to be true.

Why myths?

Why focus our attention on IR myths? Why disrupt our sacred IR stories by proclaiming them to be composed of myths? And why consider the myth function in IR theory? Is the point to rid IR theory of culture and ideology? Certainly not! Cultural practices will always mediate our encounters with the so-called 'facts' of international politics. And ideologies will always force us to consider questions of truth.

Asking questions about what makes IR theories function *as if they were true* is not the same thing as asking us to abandon our beloved myths. Nor does it amount to exposing IR myths as false because the truth or falsity of an IR myth can never be validated or invalidated. That's part of what makes it so powerful. By asking questions about the myth function in IR theory, we will not lose our precious IR myths. Rather, these IR myths bound up in IR theories will lose some of their *apparent truth*. They will return to the realms of interpretation, culture, and ideology and cease to make unopposed claims to the status of being common sense, natural, or purely empirical.

In other words, IR myths will return to the realm of the political where what they say and what they do can be analysed and debated.

By disrupting the *apparent truth* of IR myths, opportunities arise for new theories of IR to be written. Yet these, too, will be myths. So why bother interrogating the myth function in IR theory if we will never escape it? The answer to this question is in the question itself. *Because we will never escape the myth function in IR theory, we had better interrogate it.* We had better prepare ourselves to be the best critical readers of IR myths we possibly can be. Otherwise, we will just be repeating cherished stories about international relations without grasping what makes these stories *appear* to be true, without appreciating what makes them function. We will be circulating a particular way of making sense of the world without knowing how to make sense of that sense. That would make us look pretty naïve.

Plan of the book

In the following chapters, we will interrogate the myth function in IR theory by addressing three aspects of everyday IR myths.

1   What does the myth say?
    Before we can critically analyse how a myth works (its function), we must first be familiar with what the myth says (its content). We will do four things to help us understand the content of each myth:

    a   select a classic IR text that uses the myth;
    b   situate the IR text in its particular IR tradition (like realism or idealism);
    c   summarize the text;
    d   explore how the IR text makes use of the IR myth.

    For example, for the IR myth 'international anarchy is the permissive cause of war' we will do the following four things: select Kenneth Waltz's texts *Man, the State, and War* and *Theory of International Politics*, situate them in relation to the IR traditions of realism and neorealism, summarize their main arguments, and explore how they use the IR myth 'international anarchy is the permissive cause of war'.

2   How does the myth function?
    If the myth function in IR theory is to succeed, it has to be invisible. We have to forget it is even taking place, that cultural meanings are being transformed into common sense. And, in all of the IR myths explored in this book, their myth function in IR theory is extremely successful. But this presents us with a problem. How can we identify the myth function in IR theory? And how can we critically analyse the myth function in IR theory if IR theory does such a good job of explaining our world to us – to the point that we believe IR myths are true and the worlds they help to create are just the way things are?
    One answer is to think about IR theory in relation to 'other worlds'. As critical readers of myths, we are more likely to recognize and be able to interrogate myths in worlds in which we do not live – other 'cultures', other times, other

locations. But where can we find 'other worlds' that are both different enough to our own so that we can critically read the myths in them and similar enough to our own so we can identify with them enough for them to make sense to us?

My answer is to look to popular films for these 'other worlds'. Popular films provide us with ready-made, somewhat delimited 'other worlds'. In the vast cinemascapes of popular culture, there is no shortage of worlds for us to critically view. Even if a film is set in our 'culture', in our sovereign nation-state, and in our times, the world the film presents is not 'our' world, for we do not occupy this cinemascape. Yet because the film tries to depict our world, we usually understand this 'other world' and identify with it. This gap between occupying a cinematic world and identifying with it enables us to critically read 'other worlds' and the myths in them.

Another reason for turning to popular films is because they are one of the narrative spaces of visual culture. They are a way in which stories get told in visual culture. Nicholas Mirzoeff argues that 'visual culture used to be seen as a distraction from the serious business of text and history. It is now the locus of cultural and historical change' (1999:31). If that is the case, we had better learn how to read visual culture and the transformative processes that occur within it.

Accessing visual culture though popular films allows us to consider the connections between IR theory and our everyday lives. Using popular films in this way helps us to get a sense of the everyday connections between 'the popular' and 'the political'. We can see, for example, how IR myths become *everyday* IR myths – because they are circulated, received, and criticized in and through everyday, popular forms like films.

Drawing upon these ideas, we will interrogate the myth function in IR theory by doing three things:

a   select a film that illustrates the myth function in a particular IR myth;
b   summarize the film;
c   relate the film to the IR myth. Here we will ask two important questions:

• How does the film make sense of the world (Dyer, 1985)?
• What does the film say is typical and deviant in that world (Dyer, 1985)?

The popular films used to explore the myth function in IR theory are: *Lord of the Flies*, *Independence Day*, *Wag the Dog*, *Fatal Attraction*, and *The Truman Show*. *Lord of the Flies* reconsiders the realist/neorealist myth 'international anarchy is the permissive cause of war'; *Independence Day* looks at the idealist myth 'there is an international society'; *Wag the Dog* offers insights into the constructivist myth 'anarchy is what states make of it' and introduces us to the social constructivist/poststructuralist debate; *Fatal Attraction* illustrates and critiques the gender myth 'gender is a variable' while exploring the gender/feminist debate; and *The Truman Show* demonstrates how the neoliberal myth 'it is the end of history' makes neoliberal theories of globalization function at the expense of historical materialist theories of globalization.

3   What does this critical analysis of the myth function in IR theory tell us about IR theory culturally, ideologically, and popularly?

This question will be considered in the conclusion by asking two further questions that take us directly to the power politics of IR theory:

- How does IR theory make sense of the world?
- What does IR theory say is typical and deviant in that world?

These questions take us to the heart of how IR theory produces and circulates meanings about international politics. They also point to the relationships among the politics of IR theory, the politics of the popular, and the politics of storytelling.

Suggestions for further thinking

Topic 1 Mythology as methodology

Roland Barthes proposed semiology as a methodology for exploring the ideological function of myths in his book *Mythologies*. While his early work focused on exposing and putting right the 'ideological abuse' hidden in myths (and especially in 'bourgeois norms'), Barthes's later work explored more complex ways of thinking about how meanings are pluralized through reading and writing. Reading Barthes's early work on myths through his later writings, like *S/Z*, produces what Laura Kipnis calls a 'postmodernized Barthes'. It is a postmodernized Barthes whom Craig Saper constructs and deploys in his book *Artificial Mythologies*. It is a similarly postmodernized Barthes who informs my reading of IR myths. For a sense of how to apply some of these ideas to reading films, James Monaco's chapter on signs and syntax is helpful.

Suggested reading

Roland Barthes (1972) 'Myth Today', in *Mythologies*, trans. Annette Lavers. New York: Noonday Press.

—— (1974) *S/Z: An Essay*, trans. Richard Miller. New York: Hill and Wang, pp 3–16.

James Monaco (2000) 'The Language of Film: Signs and Syntax', in his *How to Read a Film*. Oxford: Oxford University Press, pp. 152–225.

Craig Saper (1997) 'Introduction' to *Artificial Mythologies*. Minneapolis: University of Minnesota Press. See also the 'Preface' by Laura Kipnis.

Topic 2 Culture, form, and IR theory

The conversation about 'cultures' is an old one in international politics, especially in those variants of international studies that tend towards what might be called 'area studies' – studies of particular regions of the world. Some very rigid ways of thinking about culture continue to be circulated in IR theory, especially in the wake of the end of the Cold War, as the essay by Samuel Huntington illustrates. Huntington's thesis is that the end of the Cold War has unleashed a clash among civilizations, grounded in their very different cultures. Pairing Huntington's essay with Edward Said's book *Orientalism* and Roxanne Doty's application of some of Said's insights to specific IR cases in her *Imperial Encounters* is one way to get students to think critically about the myths of culture and civilization Huntington constructs.

Another strain of discussions involves critical ways of thinking about culture, cultural forms, and their relationships to IR theory. Like Said's and Doty's work, some of these have been ushered into the field of international studies thanks to critical ways of thinking about identity politics. Yosef Lapid and Friedrich Krotochwil, for example, challenge IR theorists to change their conceputalizations of IR theory by 'adding' a critical conception of culture to their work. Another position, expressed by Roland Blieker, is less concerned with revising the content of IR theory through the inclusion of critical considerations of culture than it is with thinking about how different cultural forms, like poetry, offer us ways not to 'add' culture or cultural forms to IR theory but to move beyond the tired debates that traditional expressions of IR theory require. In her reading of international relations through *Star Trek*, Jutta Weldes illustrates one way in which popular cultural products like television shows and popular films allow us to approach IR theory differently.

Suggested readings

Samuel P. Huntington (1993) 'The Clash of Civilizations?', *Foreign Affairs* 72 (Summer): 22–49.

Edward Said (1978) *Orientalism: Western Conceptions of the Orient.* London: Penguin.

Roxanne Lynn Doty (1996) *Imperial Encounters: The Politics of Representation in North–South Relations.* Minneapolis: University of Minnesota Press.

Yosef Lapid and Friedrich Kratochvil (eds) (1996) *The Return of Culture and Identity in IR Theory.* Boulder, Col.: Lynne Rienner.

Roland Blieker (1997) 'Forget IR Theory', *Alternatives* 22 (1): 57–85.

Jutta Weldes (1999) 'Going Cultural: *Star Trek*, State Action, and Popular Culture', *Millennium* 28 (1): 117–34.

Chapter 2

Realism

Is international anarchy the permissive cause of war?

The claim that international politics is anarchical is almost universally embraced by IR theorists and practitioners. This is in part because the myth of international anarchy seems to describe so straightforwardly what we know about international politics. First, the anarchy myth assumes that international politics is composed of sovereign nation-states and that these sovereign nation-states are beholden to no higher power. That is what it means to be sovereign – for a state to have absolute authority over its territory and people and to have independence internationally. In international theory, all states in international politics are assumed to be sovereign, even though there are debates about degrees and/or kinds of sovereignty (Jackson, 1990). And while some IR theorists consider sovereignty itself to be a myth (Biersteker and Weber, 1996), most regard it as the primary fact of international political life.

The second 'fact' of international political life – and the second assumption of the anarchy myth – is that there is no world government. This is why sovereign nation-states are beholden to no higher power. There just is no higher power than that of a sovereign nation-state. Because there is no higher power that a state *must* obey, states are said to have international independence. This is so even if a state joins an international organization like the UN or NATO. This does not impinge upon a state's sovereignty or international independence because state membership in these organizations is voluntary. So a state can quit an organization if it wants to.

Combining the absence of world government with state sovereignty, many IR theorists conclude that international politics is anarchical. But this conclusion only makes sense if one more assumption is made. This third assumption has to do with the meaning of anarchy. In political theory, 'anarchy' denotes a lack of order. We usually describe states experiencing civil wars as anarchical, for example. But in international theory 'anarchy' denotes a *lack of an orderer* – someone or something who/which self-consciously imposes order in a top-down way on to sovereign nation-states. So in international theory anarchy prevails even if there is order (like power-balancing among sovereign nation-states or one hegemonic state being able to call most of the shots like the US does). These sorts of 'order' are still considered to be anarchical because there is no world government (see Box 2.1).

There are countless versions of the anarchy myth, each with a very different way of describing and mythologizing the 'realities' of international anarchy. Yet of all of these anarchy myths, the one that is the best known and the most widely accepted is Kenneth Waltz's myth 'international anarchy is the permissive cause of war', a myth that dates back to 1954.

Why is Waltz's myth 'international anarchy is the permissive cause of war' so

---

Box 2.1 Three assumptions of the international anarchy myth

1 International politics is composed of sovereign nation-states
2 There is no world government, which means there is no international orderer
3 The absence of a world government or orderer by definition means that international politics is anarchical

---

influential? And why has it endured nearly half a century? One reason is that it does more than make anarchy the context in which sovereign nation-states carry out their day-to-day politics. In Waltz's anarchy myth, international anarchy becomes the answer to the question that spawned IR theory as an academic discipline after WWI. That question is 'Why do wars occur?' By causally linking international anarchy to war, Waltz did more to popularize the anarchy myth than any other IR theorist before him or since.

Another reason is that Waltz's anarchy myth has been theorized from the perspectives of both realism and new or neorealism (see Table 2.1). Both realism and neorealism accept the three fundamental assumptions that make the anarchy myth function – first, that the world is composed of sovereign nation-states; second, that there is no world government which means there is no international orderer; and third, that the absence of world government or an international orderer by definition means that international politics is anarchical. From these three elements, realists and neorealists both predict that sovereign nation-states in a system of international anarchy will behave conflictually. While individual wars may be stopped from time to time, war itself cannot be transcended. But why?

Realists and neorealists agree that the overriding goal of states in this environment of international anarchy is to survive. This is their overriding interest. And the only way that states can reasonably ensure their survival is to increase their power. Power protects states because states with less power might fear those with more power and therefore be less likely to attack them.

Additionally, realists and neorealists agree that there is no way out of international anarchy. It is *un*realistic to think that a world government could be formed because states would never be secure enough – and therefore trusting enough – to give up their power to a world government.

With all this in common, what do realists and neorealists disagree about? One thing they disagree about is the issue of human nature. Realists like Hans Morgenthau, for example, argue that the nature of man (and he meant the gender-exclusive term 'man'; see Tickner, 1992: Chapter 2) is fundamentally flawed. In Morgenthau's account, man may not be purely evil, but he is certainly tainted by original sin. And that means that pessimism about how man and groups of men (organized into sovereign nation-states) will behave is the only realistic way to approach international politics. At its root, then, international politics will remain anarchical and conflictual because of the nature of man.

Neorealists, of whom Kenneth Waltz was the first, disagree. They argue that instead of looking to 'natural' causes of conflict, we need to look to 'social' ones instead. Following Jean-Jacques Rousseau, Waltz argues that the organization of social relations rather than the nature of man is what determines whether or not we have war. Why? Because good men behave badly in bad social organizations, and bad men can be stopped from behaving badly if they are in good social organizations. States go to war, then, because they are in a bad social organization. And Waltz calls that bad social organization international anarchy. 'International anarchy is the permissive cause of war.' So, realists and neorealists differ on how they conceptualize international anarchy. For realists, it is just the environment in which sovereign nation-states act. For neorealists, international anarchy describes the social relations among sovereign nation-states that causally explain why wars occur.

Table 2.1 Realism vs. neorealism

	Realism	*Neorealism*
Interest of states	*Survival*	*Survival*
How to achieve survival	Increase power because world government unachievable	Increase power because world government unachievable
Human nature	Man is flawed and therefore prone to conflict. This explains why cooperation is never guaranteed and world government is unachievable	Man may or may not be flawed. Human nature is not essential to an explanation of conflict
Anarchy	The environment in which sovereign nation-states act	Describes the social relations among sovereign nation-states that causally explain why wars occur

In this chapter, I will consider the myth 'international anarchy is the permissive cause of war' and the specific uses Kenneth Waltz makes of this myth. I will do so by examining what have become two of the most famous books about IR theory, both authored by Waltz. In the first, *Man, the State, and War* (first published in 1954), Waltz makes his famous argument that 'international anarchy is the permissive cause of war'. In the second, *Theory of International Politics* (1979), Waltz extends international anarchy from a cause of war into a systemic ordering principle of the international system, a move which gives birth to the tradition of neorealism. I will summarize the arguments Waltz makes in each of these books, relate his arguments to the myth 'international anarchy is the permissive cause of war', and reconsider the myth function of Waltz's arguments about international anarchy through the film *Lord of the Files*.

Lord of the Flies tells a story about moving from one type of order (hierarchy) into another (anarchy), suggesting that anarchy is what allows conflict to occur. As such, it illustrates the arguments Waltz makes in his two books. Yet *Lord of the Flies* also offers insights into what makes Waltz's anarchy myth function by showing us how fear is both a crucial and an externalized component of Waltz's anarchy myth (Ashley, 1989). Without fear, Waltz's arguments fail to be persuasive. What would international politics be like if fear functioned differently from the way it does in Waltz's myth? What would this mean for IR theory? These are the sorts of questions a functional analysis of Waltz's work allows us to consider.

What does the myth say?

Why do wars occur? This is the question Kenneth Waltz asked himself in the early 1950s. Waltz's question is as old as war itself, possibly because 'to explain how peace can be more readily achieved requires an understanding of the causes of war' (Waltz, 1959:2). By the time Waltz posed this question, many answers to it already existed. These answers fell into three categories (or, as IR theorists came to define them, were found at the three 'levels of analysis' or in the 'three images'). These three categories/levels/images are: the individual, the state, and the state system. In *Man, the State, and War*, Waltz argued that the major causes of war are to be found at each of these levels of analysis, with none of them alone being sufficient to explain why wars do or do not occur.

How did Waltz come to this conclusion? Waltz began by looking at the first category/level/image – man. For Waltz, as for so many other IR theorists, the term 'man' denotes the individual level and particularly an interest in human nature, forgetting of course that not all individuals are men. The first image explanation of war goes like this:

> the locus of the important causes of war is found in the nature and behavior of man. War results from selfishness, from misdirected aggressive impulses, from stupidity. . . . If these are the primary causes of war, then the elimination of war must come through uplifting and enlightening men or securing their psychic-social readjustment.
>
> (Waltz, 1959:16)

This is the 'men behaving badly' explanation of war. Man behaves badly because he is bad by nature. He acts unreasonably or he prioritizes selfish goals over communitarian goals, and this is why conflicts and wars occur. This is the sort of 'natural man' realist IR scholars invoke to explain the recurrence and repetition of wars. But, as idealist IR theorists point out, men do not always behave badly (see Chapter 3). Some men seem to be good by nature – they act reasonably to pursue the common good. There is a fundamental goodness to man, and if that fundamental goodness could be universalized – if all men could access their fundamental goodness – then all men could behave well. Conflicts and wars could be averted altogether.

In reviewing these pessimistic and optimistic descriptions of the nature of man, Waltz noted a couple of problems. First, he suggested that the 'causal importance of human nature' is generally exaggerated by all human-nature theorists. Can we really say that human nature *alone* causes war? Not for Waltz, for how can pessimists explain why wars don't occur all the time and how can optimists explain why they occur some of the time? Human-nature explanations of war don't seem to account for variations in the presence or absence of war. And, anyway, don't good men as well as bad men sometimes make war? Waltz concludes that human nature is too complex to be so directly and causally linked to war as the sole explanation for why wars occur (Waltz, 1959:40).

Second, this insufficiency of human nature to explain the presence or absence of war means that we must look to social and political institutions to supplement our understanding of why wars occur. For example, if human nature cannot be changed – whether it is always good or bad – then we cannot decrease the occurrence of war by trying to change it. All we can do is look to social and political institutions that do change and try to change them to decrease the likelihood of war. Conversely, if human nature can be changed, then we still need to look to social and political institutions because human nature would be changed through interactions with these institutions. All this leads Waltz to conclude that human nature itself is never sufficient to explain the presence or absence of war. It must be supplemented by an analysis of social and political institutions. This leads Waltz to investigate second-level/image explanations of the causes of war.

At the second level of analysis, Waltz asks whether the occurrence of wars can be explained by the internal organization of states and societies. Just as first-image theorists argue there are good and bad men, second-image theorists argue there are good and bad states, either because of their formal governmental arrangements (democratic vs. autocratic, for example; see Chapter 3) or their less formal social arrangements (who owns the means of production; see Chapter 6). Like first-image analyses, second-image theories claim that bad actors (this time states) make war, and good actors preserve the peace. But, as before, these sorts of explanations raise critical questions for Waltz. For example, if bad states make war, what will change bad states to good states? (Waltz, 1959:114). Not surprisingly, there is no agreement among second-image theorists on just what to do. Some suggest good states would be democratic, others say they should be monarchical, others still say socialist (Waltz, 1959:120). And, Waltz suggests, even if second-image theorists could agree on what a good state was, there is still no guarantee that a world of 'good states' would be a peaceful world. Like 'good men', 'good states' sometimes make war.

Once again, Waltz concludes that this level of analysis is incomplete. This state level needs to be supplemented by the international level, for, as Waltz puts it, 'the international political environment has much to do with the ways in which states behave' (Waltz, 1959:122–3). And this leads Waltz to consider the third level of analysis or third image in his quest to understand why wars occur.

Waltz summarizes the third image as follows: 'With many sovereign states, with no system of law enforceable among them, with each state judging its grievances and ambitions according to the dictates of its own reason or desire – conflict, sometimes leading to war, is bound to occur' (Waltz, 1959:159). It is worth quoting a somewhat lengthy passage by Waltz in which he details the linkages between anarchy, state actions, and conflict.

> In anarchy there is no automatic harmony. . . . A state will use force to attain its goals if, after assessing the prospects for success, it values those goals more than it values the pleasures of peace. Because each state is the final judge of its own cause, any state may at any time use force to implement its policies. Because any state may at any time use force, all states must constantly be ready either to counter force with force or to pay the cost of weakness. The requirements of state action are, in this view, imposed by the circumstances in which all states exist.
>
> (Waltz, 1959:160)

In a situation of international anarchy as Waltz describes it, no 'supreme authority' like an international government can stop states from forcefully pursuing their own interests. Waltz concludes that 'war occurs because there is nothing to prevent it' (Waltz, 1959:188). This is why he describes international anarchy 'as a permissive or underlying cause of war' (Waltz, 1959:232).

As a permissive cause of war, international anarchy is also the limit on states' abilities to cooperate with one another. Because there is no one to enforce cooperation, states will act in their own self-interests rather than in the interests of the state system. Waltz elaborates this point with reference to the parable of the stag hunt, told by Jean-Jacques Rousseau.

> Assume that five men who have acquired a rudimentary ability to speak and to understand each other happen to come together at a time when all of them suffer from hunger. The hunger of each will be satisfied by the fifth part of stag, so they 'agree' to co-operate in a project to trap one. But also the hunger of any one of them will be satisfied by a hare, so, as a hare comes within reach, one of them grabs it. The defector obtains the means of satisfying his hunger but in doing so permits the stag to escape. His immediate interest prevails over consideration for his fellows.
>
> (Waltz, 1959:167–8)

So, for Waltz, international anarchy explains both why wars ultimately may occur and why there are limits on cooperation among states in the international system. Without a leader to punish a hunter who defected from the stag hunt or an international government to punish a rogue state, cooperation can never be guaranteed and conflict is always a serious possibility.

Yet even though Waltz argues that only international anarchy has the power to explain why wars *may* occur, he stresses that individual and state-level factors still need to be considered when we think about why specific wars *do* occur. For Waltz, the first and second images constitute the immediate causes of war. If individuals and states do not pursue war-like policies or do not pursue selfish interests that could not also be understood as in the general interest of all states, then, even though the third image of international anarchy permits the occurrence of war, there would be no war (Waltz, 1959:238).

Another way to put it is like this: if individuals and states have nothing to *fear* from one another, then they have no cause to fight wars with one another. Something in addition to international anarchy is always required to explain why we move from a situation in which wars may occur to a situation in which wars *do* occur. Overall, then, in *Man, the State, and War*, Waltz argues that all three images need to be considered together to determine whether or not wars will occur (see Table 2.2). And because Waltz locates the immediate causes of war in either individual men or states understood as collective men, realists are able to embrace his myth 'international anarchy is the permissive cause of war'.

Table 2.2 Causes of war for Waltz

Location	Description	Type of cause
First image	Nature of man	Immediate
Second image	International organization of states and societies	Immediate
Third image	International anarchy	Permissive

Theory of International Politics might be described as a book in which Waltz both builds upon and forgets much of what he wrote in *Man, the State, and War*. What Waltz builds upon is the weight which he gives to international anarchy in explaining international conflict. What he forgets is to include first- and second-image explanations in his analysis of why wars occur. In this later book, then, there are no serious discussions of individuals or of the internal arrangements of states and society. Sovereign nation-states are Waltz's principal actors, but instead of the complexity they had in *Man, the State, and War*, Waltz now discusses them as (at worst) billiard balls that knock one another around or (at best) firms that freely compete with one another in the international system (Waltz, 1979:91).

To be fair to Waltz, *Theory of International Politics* is not meant to have the wide sweep of *Man, the State, and War*. Waltz claims that this later book is concerned only with elaborating the workings of the international level. But this later book is in some ways not just an extension of the earlier book. This is because instead of arguing that an understanding of the international requires an understanding of individual and state-level factors as he did in *Man, the State, and War*, Waltz elevates his third image of international anarchy into a principle that at times seems to be downright determinist. International anarchy has much more explanatory purchase in *Theory of International Politics* than it had in *Man, the State, and War*. International anarchy seems to dictate how states in the state system must behave, rather than suggest (as it did in his earlier book) how they *might* behave. This is because in *Theory of International Politics* international anarchy becomes the structural ordering principle of international politics, from which all state behaviours seem to flow. As a result, *Theory of International Politics* marks a clear break between realism and neorealism.

Without getting into too much dry detail, Waltz's argument in *Theory of International Politics* is this (summarized in Table 2.3). The behaviour of actors in a system depends upon how they are organized. The two major forms of organization that matter for politics are hierarchy and anarchy. Hierarchy describes how politics is organized within states – with a clear centre that has a monopoly on the legitimate uses of power and a distribution of labour among various branches of government. Anarchy describes how politics is organized globally, between states in the international system – with no clear centre of power, significant power held by at least two states (or poles as they are called in IR theory), and each state functioning like every other state in international politics because there is no division of labour to speak of among states.

Waltz argues that these different structures of hierarchy and anarchy – these different ways of organizing political power – result in different consequences for actors. Again, actors will behave differently depending upon how they are organized. So, for example, within a domestic, hierarchical organization, political processes can be specialized because there are different branches and levels of government, these various government sectors are all highly interdependent upon one another, and their overriding goal is to maximize the welfare of the citizens of their states. In contrast, within a global, anarchical organization, states cannot be specialized because there is just one state doing all the tasks. Therefore, rather than specializing, states in the state system imitate one another's behaviours. They attempt to be as independent of other states as they can be, and they strive to maximize their own international security (Waltz, 1979: Chapter 5).

Table 2.3 Waltzian neorealism

| | Structure | | |
	Ordering principle	Formal differentiation	Distribution of power
Domestic	• Hierarchy • Centred	• Heterogeneous • Dissimilar	Monopoly
Global	• Anarchy • Decentred	Heterogeneous	Oligopoly

| | Consequences | | |
	Political processes	Relationships	Goals
Domestic	Specialization	High interdependence	Maximize welfare
Global	• Imitation • Balancing	Low interdependence	Maximize security

What this means for the everyday practices of states is that, domestically, states strive to make life as good as they can for their citizens. Quality-of-life issues prevail domestically, and, importantly, they can prevail because security issues are mostly solved within states. Certainly, crimes and sometimes rebellions occur, but there is a general agreement within a state as to where authority resides and therefore who can exercise power. With security issues muted within states, states can focus on welfare issues.

In contrast, Waltz argues, security issues are never solved within the state system. Because there is no orderer – because international anarchy prevails – there is never anything or anyone to prevent conflicts from occurring. States are forced to look out for their own interests. The overriding interest of a state is to survive – to carry on being a state. And, Waltz argues, in a situation of structural anarchy, the best chance states have for surviving is to maximize their power. Sure, states could all give up their power to some world government and transform international anarchy into international hierarchy. Then states could cease to worry about security issues and focus on issues of international welfare. But, Waltz (who is often called a structural, new, or neorealist) agrees with other realists that this is a utopian pipe dream. It isn't going to happen. And, even if it did, then we'd be discussing what happens in hierarchical structures, whereas the point of Waltz's *Theory of International Politics* is to elaborate what happens in anarchical structures.

In international anarchy, because all states recognize that it is in their over-riding self-interest to maximize their power, that's what Waltz says they do. To do anything else is crazy because a state without enough power is a vulnerable state. And, anyway, it is too scary for states not to try to maximize their power. This is what Waltz calls the 'security dilemma'. He argues that when one state sees another state trying to increase its power to increase its security, it gets scared, feels threatened, and recognizes that it too must increase its power. But, of course, that scares the other states, and basically there is this mad spiral in which all states are trying to have more power than all other states. According to Waltz, this competition for power among states is not always as dangerous as it at first sounds. It doesn't have to lead to war, so long as no state has significantly more power than another state or coalition of states, so long as states in combination are in a stable 'balance of power' arrangement.

But power does not always balance out like this. Waltz argues that power is most likely to balance out in this way when there are only two poles – when there is a bipolar system. When there are more then two poles, things get trickier. Balances are harder to strike. Risks increase. Wars are more likely to occur. International anarchy remains the permissive cause of war (Waltz, 1979: Chapter 6).

Overall, Waltz's two books mythologize international anarchy as the permissive cause of war. The first book explicitly links anarchy to war, while the second book explains state behaviour – whether conflictual or merely competitive – from the first principle of international anarchy. And both books reserve a place for fear as what either explains the immediate causes of war (men or states behaving badly) or the seemingly inevitable behaviours of states locked into a competition for power in international anarchy.

The film *Lord of the Flies* cleverly plays with these themes of good and bad individuals, good and bad 'states', and differing forms of organization (hierarchy vs. anarchy). As such, it nicely illustrates many of the points Waltz makes in his two books. But, most importantly for our purposes, *Lord of the Flies* invites us to reconsider the use Waltz makes of fear in his analyses of international anarchy. In *Man, the State, and War*, states may fear one another because of the bad behaviour of either ruling individuals or rogue states. Fear, in other words, is located in the first or second image. But by the time we get to *Theory of International Politics*, fear seems to be located in the third image – in international anarchy itself because it is anarchy that makes states behave as they do (to maximize their power) and it is consequently this behaviour that leads other states to fear them.

Lord of the Flies explores all of these locations of fear, while suggesting one more. Maybe fear is not something fixed in one or more levels of analysis. Maybe fear is not a consequence of state behaviour in a system of structural anarchy. Instead, maybe fear is something that is actually missing in a situation of international anarchy, and because it is missing it must be invented and skillfully deployed. Put differently, maybe fear is the final supplement or addition to Waltz's myth that 'international anarchy is the permissive cause of war', a supplement not necessarily found in *any* of his three images (Ashley, 1989).

Lord of the Flies

The film *Lord of the Flies* is based on William Golding's novel of the same name which was published in 1954, the same year Waltz's *Man, the State, and War* was published. The 1963 British film version of the novel, directed by Peter Brook, was re-released in the British Classics video series in 1999. An American version, directed by Harry Hook, was released in 1994. The American film version makes several critical deviations from Golding's novel that present obstacles to rethinking Waltz's anarchy myth through it (see 'Note on the American film *Lord of the Flies*', p. 34). In contrast, the British film follows Golding's novel more closely and, it must be said, is simply a more powerful presentation of the story. It is for these reasons that I will focus my attention on the British 1963 film.

Lord of the Flies is set during WWII when the UK was being bombed by Germany. Because of the heavy bombing experienced by many English cities, a mass exodus of British children was organized – some to the British countryside and others out of the UK altogether. Such is the plight of the British school boys (aged about 5 to 12) we encounter in the film. They are presumably being flown from war-torn Britain to Australia when their plane crashes on a remote, uninhabited Pacific island. No adults survive the crash.

The opening photomontage and soundtrack depict the boys' transition from life in England to life on the island. In it are seen and heard the sights and sounds of English school life – boys in a class photo, at their desks, in the dining hall, in chapel, playing cricket, and teachers organizing their activities and watching over them. Then, abruptly, the pace at which images and sounds are introduced quickens, and we see and hear missile launches, war planes, and bombing raids violently inserted into the montage. Finally, we see photos of the boys' planned evacuation, their plane caught in a storm, a map of the Pacific, and the plane crashing near an island. The photomontage ends, and the action begins.

This opening starkly introduces the two worlds of *Lord of the Flies* – the lost world of hierarchy from which the boys have just exited and the island world of anarchy they have just entered. Hierarchy is marked by rules, reason, law and order, all of which are ensured (at least from the boys' point of view) by the presence of grown-ups. Anarchy is unmarked as the film opens. The film is the story of how the boys behave in a situation of anarchy, in a world without adults (see Table 2.4).

How *Lord of the Flies* makes sense of the world is by exploring what happens to boys when they move from one world (the world of school/home/nation-state) into another world (the lost island world). What these two worlds represent is a reversal of what the boys are accustomed to as typical and deviant. In the familiar world of school/home/nation-state, what is typical of the world is hierarchy and what is deviant in that world is anarchy. But in the lost island world the boys now find themselves inhabiting, anarchy is typical and hierarchy is deviant (see Table 2.5). How will the boys cope in this deviant, new world of anarchy?

Not surprisingly, the boy's first coping strategy is an attempt to create hierarchy within anarchy. There may be no grown-ups on the island, but that does not mean there has to be an absence of civilized order. As one of the boys puts it, 'We've got to have rules and obey them. After all, we're not savages. We're English, and the English

Table 2.4 How does *Lord of the Flies* represent hierarchy and anarchy?

Hierarchy	Anarchy
Characterized by rules, reason, law and order, all of which are guaranteed by the presence of adults	Characterized by the absence of guarantees to order or reason because of the absence of adults

Table 2.5 What is typical and what is deviant in the two worlds of *Lord of the Flies*?

	Familiar world	Island world
Typical	Hierarchy	Anarchy
Deviant	Anarchy	Hierarchy

are best at everything. So we've got to do the right things.' The boys are not only all English. They are all English school boys. This means that even though the boys are from different schools (indicated by their different uniforms), they have an implicit if not explicit knowledge of social codes that can be mobilized to create and sustain organizing hierarchies. And this is precisely what the boys draw upon to establish their new order.

The boys elect Ralph as their leader. Ralph is the boy who was responsible for bringing all the stranded boys on the island together by blowing into a conch shell as one would blow on a trumpet. The conch becomes the symbol of rules and rights. Whoever holds the conch at assembly has the right to speak and be heard. Jack, the leader of a group of choir boys from one school, is the only boy who could really challenge Ralph's leadership. Ralph wisely gives Jack control over his choir, and Jack (who seems to be the only boy on the island in possession of a knife) decides that they will be hunters. Piggy, the voice of reason from the old world, is responsible for taking names and minding the little ones. These jobs suit Piggy for, as his name implies, he is physically unfit for much else.

Life goes on rather blissfully for some time. Images of happy boys working together to build shelters, playing games and gathering fruit fill the screen. Jack's boys amuse themselves by exploring the island and trying to kill wild boar. However they spend their time, all the boys agree that they have one overriding goal in common – to be rescued. They decide to build a fire on the mountain top that they will keep going so a plane or a ship might see them. Jack volunteers his hunters for this job. The rules seem to be well in place, and everyone seems to be working within them for the common good.

All proceeds well until one day a plane flies overhead, and Ralph and the other boys on the beach realize that the fire has gone out. Jack's hunters are euphoric because they have killed their first wild boar. But because of their increased attention to their 'need for meat', they have neglected to uphold their part of the bargain – keeping the fire alight. Jack's boys have shifted their priorities. The film represents this change both visually and musically. Visually, Jack appears increasingly warrior-like as the film proceeds – first with his knife, then his spear, and finally with his painted face. Musically, the peaceful, civilized music Jack's choir sang as they first entered the film gives way over the course of the film to a drummed, war-like rendition of their Latin song. In many scenes, a chant about hunting and killing unites Jack's choir/hunters, and not their original song.

It is not surprising that goals would diverge and agreements would be abandoned in the absence of an orderer. As Waltz would remind us, in a situation of structural anarchy, there is nothing or no one to enforce the rules or common goals. Yet, at this stage anyway, there is an orderer, and that orderer is Ralph. He was

Plate 2.1 Ralph blows the conch shell to call the stranded school boys to assembly.
© Canal + Image UK Ltd., courtesy of the British Film Institute

elected chief by the other boys. But his interests and those of Jack begin to conflict. Jack is interested in hunting, a skill that will help the boys survive on the island. This is his immediate reality and his immediate aim. In contrast, Ralph is more interested in the longer-term possibility of rescue because he does not believe the boys can survive indefinitely on the island.

As the film proceeds, this conflict of interests is exacerbated until the hierarchy of Ralph as elected chief breaks down because Jack directly challenges him. The challenge begins when Ralph tries to protect Piggy's right to speak because Piggy is holding the conch.

Jack interrupts Piggy: Shut up you fat slug.
Ralph: Jack, let him speak. He's got the conch!
Jack: And you shut up you. Who are you anyway just sitting there telling people what to do? You can't hunt, you can't sing.
Ralph: I'm chief. I was chosen.
Jack: Why should choosing make any difference, telling people what to do?
Ralph: The rules, you're breaking the rules.
Jack: Who cares!
Ralph: Because the rules are the only thing we got.
Jack: Bullocks to the rules.

Plate 2.2 Jack's choir boys.
© Canal + Image UK Ltd., courtesy of the British Film Institute.

In this scene, Ralph is right. Indeed, he is too right for his own good. The rules are all the boys have of the hierarchy they attempt to create in this world without grown-ups. But because they don't have any grown-ups – because they don't have anyone whose authority is unchallenged on account of their structural position – there is no way to enforce the rules. As Jack proves in this scene, the rules mean nothing without the power of enforcement.

It isn't long after this that the hierarchy the boys cling to unravels altogether. Jack leaves the group, going off on his own. He is eventually joined by Roger (a hunter) and then the rest of the hunters. Increasingly, the boys break up into two distinct societies on the island – those organized around the principle of rescue who work at keeping the fire going and those organized around the principle of survival who spend their time hunting wild boar. As time goes on, almost all of the boys join Jack's 'tribe'. He gives them food. He offers them protection.

And things get even worse from this point. Not only are the boys divided over what goals to prioritize, but they end up in deadly conflict with one another. It seems to begin with the humiliation of Ralph and Piggy. They are fed bananas when they have asked to share the meat of a kill, underscoring their weakness. Then Jack and his boys steal Piggy's glasses, thereby taking control of the fire and leaving Ralph and Piggy nothing immediate to offer the others, apart from the fading possibility of rescue. When Ralph and Piggy go to Jack's end of the island in an attempt to get

Piggy's glasses back, Jack and his tribe treat them badly by taunting and threatening them. And then Roger intentionally pushes a rock over the cliff, killing Piggy (the voice of hierarchical reason) who is holding the conch (the symbol of rules and order). Ralph runs away, only to be eventually hunted by Jack and his tribe.

Jack's tribe smoke Ralph out of the forest by setting it on fire. Ralph scrambles through the forest, pursued by Jack's boys, as their hunting chants grow louder and louder in Ralph's head. Eventually, he makes his way to the beach. He falls at the feet of a British naval officer, who has come to investigate the island because of the massive fire. The soundtrack falls silent, as Ralph and the boys pursuing him try to comprehend their situation. The camera focuses on the naval officer and his crew. The soundtrack plays again, this time a trumpet arrangement of the original choir music so sweetly sung by Jack's boys earlier. Anarchy gives way to hierarchy. Order is restored. The stunned boys prepare to reenter the world of enforceable hierarchy that they left so long ago.

Lord of the Flies seems to make a pretty good case for Waltz's myth that 'international anarchy is the permissive cause of war' and that in a world of structural anarchy the necessary pursuit of survival in this self-help world may well lead to conflict. Whether one goes with Waltz's thesis in *Man, the State, and War*, that an immediate cause of war like human nature (a first-image problem) or bad social organization (a second-image problem) is needed to supplement international anarchy, or his thesis in *Theory of International Politics*, that the structure of anarchy is enough to explain why competition among actors will occur, thereby leading to the possibility of either balancing or war, *Lord of the Flies* seems to support his myth that 'international anarchy is the permissive cause of war'.

The film takes us through five moves that support Waltz's myth. First, there is the loss of hierarchy (no adults). Second, there is the attempt to reimpose hierarchy with rules and elections. Third, hierarchy fails because there is no one to enforce the rules. Fourth, conflict breaks out among the boys, resulting in a war between the two groups and the intentional killing of Piggy. Finally, anarchy ends with the reintroduction of adult authority. Even though this is where the film ends, we know that the behaviour the boys exhibited on the island will not match their behaviour in the world of adults. The music, if nothing else, confirms this.

As compelling a case as this may be for Waltz's thesis, there is a crucial move missing from the above list – a move that puts Waltz's thesis about anarchy into doubt. For, as this missing move demonstrates, it is not just the lack of hierarchy that leads to conflict or that makes it possible. What is missing from this list and what is clearly illustrated in the film is the supplemental function of fear in Waltz's anarchy myth. Without fear, the move from hierarchy to anarchy is not *necessarily* the move from the ability to prevent war to the inability to prevent war (see Box 2.2).

As *Lord of the Flies* tells the story of the boys' departure from hierarchy and their making sense of their lives in anarchy – marking anarchy first by cooperation and then by conflict – it also tells a parallel story about the boys' increasing fear. Certainly, there is the fear of being on an uninhabited island in the aftermath of a plane crash without any adults. But in addition to this rational fear, the film introduces more and more irrational fear. Initially, this fear is something held by the little boys. One of them asks early on what the bigger boys are going to do about the 'snake-thing'.

> **Box 2.2 Where does fear figure in Waltz's myth as enacted in *Lord of the Flies*?**
>
> Loss of hierarchy
> (symbolized by lack of adults)
>
> Reestabilishment of hierarchy with rules and election
> (symbolized by conch shell)
>
> *Fear becomes widespread among boys*
> *(symbolized by their belief in the beast)*
> **This is what goes without saying in Waltz's myth.**
>
> Hierarchy fails
> (symbolized by Jack leaving the group and starting a rival group)
>
> Conflict occurs
> (Jack's and Ralph's groups fight/Piggy is killed)
>
> Anarchy ends
> (symbolized by the rescue of the boys and the reintroduction of adults)

Ralph: The snake-thing?

Piggy [into whose ear the little boy is speaking for Piggy to speak for him at the assembly]:   Now he says it was a beastie.

Ralph: Beastie? [He and the other boys laugh.]

Piggy: A snake-thing, ever so big. He saw it.

Ralph: When?

Piggy: When he was hiding in the jungle in the dark. He says, 'When the rain stopped, it turned into one of them things like ropes in the trees and hung in the branches.' He says, 'Will it come back tonight?'

The boys look scared.

Ralph: But there isn't a beastie. I tell you, there isn't a beast.

Jack: Ralph's right, of course. There isn't a snake-thing. But if there was, we'd hunt and kill it.

In this scene, the beast is introduced by a little boy, and its existence is denied by both Ralph and Jack. But there is a critical difference between how Ralph and Jack deal with the existence of a beast. Ralph sticks firmly to the argument that there is no beast. Jack, in contrast, seems to agree with Ralph, yet he leaves open the possibility that there is a beast by saying that 'if there was, we'd hunt and kill it'. Something that does not exist does not need to be hunted and killed.

It is Jack, not a little boy, who next brings up the beast. He does so when he defends his hunters for their neglect of the fire when the plane passed overhead. He tells the boys at assembly:

Jack: We're hunters. And if there is a beast, it is my hunters who will protect you from it.

Jack leans down to a little boy, Percival, who Jack then speaks for.

Jack: He says the beast comes out of the sea.

The boys look scared.

Another boy: My daddy said they hadn't found all the animals in the sea. My daddy said there are animals – what do you call them – that make ink and are hundreds of feet long and eat whales whole.

Someone else shouts: A squid can't come out of the water.

Another boy: Maybe he means it's some kind of ghost.

Another boy: Maybe that's what the beast is – some kind of ghost.

Piggy: I don't believe in no ghosts, ever.

Jack: Who cares what you believe, fatty. (Laughter)

Simon: Maybe there is a beast . . . What I mean is, maybe it's only us.

Someone: Nuts.

Ralph: We should have left this 'til daylight. We're tired. We'll have a vote – on ghosts I mean. And then we'll go back to the shelters. Who thinks there may be ghosts?

Almost all the boys raise their hands.

While Jack is increasingly using the beast as a way to shift the boys' priorities from being rescued on the island to surviving on the island, the fear of the beast has spread from just the little boys to almost all of the boys. And, as Jack realizes, encouraging the boys' belief in and fear of the beast is a good way to challenge Ralph's authority. It is *after* this meeting that Jack says bullocks to the rules, that the hierarchy the boys created on this anarchical island turns competitive rather than cooperative.

Soon after this meeting, the twins Sam and Eric think they see the beast on a mountain top. They saw something swaying in the breeze. They say that as they ran down the mountain the beast followed them and nearly caught them. Jack cries, 'We'll hunt it.'

Jack, Ralph, and a group of bigger boys go to hunt the beast. The hunt lasts until after dark, when the boys arrive on the mountain top and see 'the beast'. They run down the mountain screaming. The 'truth' of the beast has now been established. It is only *after* the beast seems to move from fiction to fact that Jack gets fed up with Ralph's rules about fires and rescue and leaves the group, to be joined eventually by his hunters and most of the other boys.

One day, after Jack's tribe has killed another wild boar, Jack cuts off the boar's head and leaves it as a gift for the beast. As Jack and his tribe celebrate their kill late into the night, Simon (who earlier said that the beast could be 'us') climbs up the mountain and comes face to face with the beast, without fear. He discovers that 'the beast' is a dead paratrooper hanging from a tree. This is why he appears to move. And his parachute is swaying in the breeze. This is what Sam and Eric saw. Simon descends the mountain in the dark. Jack's tribe is celebrating wildly, chanting 'kill the beast, cut his throat, spill his blood'. They see something move in the brush. Someone says, 'It's the beast,' and the boys kill it. Of course, it is Simon.

Simon must die because he is the one who has the knowledge that there is no beast, and without a beast, it would be harder for Jack to make his claim to leadership against Ralph. For survival seems extremely urgent when there is a threat. Ralph is

Plate 2.3 Jack transformed from head choir boy into tribal leader.
© Canal + Image UK Ltd., courtesy of the British Film Institute.

no threat. Piggy is no threat. The few little boys they look after are no threat. But the beast is a 'real' threat. The beast is what is necessary to make a threat to survival seem real. And even killing Simon, who Jack claims was the beast in disguise, is not enough to kill the beast. Jack makes this clear as his tribe prepares for another hunt.

Jack: Tomorrow I'll hunt again. Then we'll leave another head for the beast. Some of you will stay and defend the gate. The beast may try to come in. Remember how he crawled. He came disguised. The beast may try and come, even though we gave him the head of our kill. So watch, and be careful.
Boy: But didn't we. . . . Didn't we. . . .
Jack: No, how could we kill it?
Another boy: He told us. The beast was disguised.

The beast – or the fear it represents – can never be killed because it is a necessary fear. It is necessary for Waltz's anarchy myth to function.

The function of fear in Waltz's anarchy myth

Lord of the Flies illustrates not only the seeming truth of Waltz's anarchy myth – 'international anarchy is the permissive cause of war' – but it also shows us what makes Waltz's myth function. As the film illustrates, anarchy alone is insufficient to cause or even allow for conflict. Anarchy requires fear to differentiate the behaviour of those acting within it from their behaviour within hierarchy. The absence of adults symbolizes the move from hierarchy to anarchy in the film. But hierarchy persists in the absence of adults *until fear is introduced*. Without fear, there is nothing in the film or in Waltz's myth that suggests that anarchy would be conflictual rather than cooperative.

As the film illustrates, fear can be found in any of Waltz's three images. The way Golding's novel is often read is as a testimony to the evilness of human nature that comes out in extreme situations. Man is by nature evil. The rules are all we've got. We had better cling to the rules to avoid behaving like beasts in a state of nature. This is one way to interpret Simon's declaration that the beast may only be us. One can make the case that Jack, especially, is lured to some initial savage state of man. It is because of his increasing irrationality and how seductively he presents this irrationality as rational on the island that is the immediate cause of conflict among the boys. Read in this way, fear is a first-image problem.

But, of course, Golding's story is an analogy for what is happening among sovereign nation-states during WWII. States, too, are behaving badly. Germany is taking over Europe and bombing the UK. Because there is no world government to mediate the Allieds/Axis dispute, WWII occurs. Jack's tribe can be read as a bad organization that spreads conflict rather than adhering to the initially agreed upon goal of rescue through cooperative fire building. Because there is no adult to prevent disputes between Jack's wild survivalists and Ralph's rational rescue wannabes, Jack's tribe and Ralph's group come into conflict. This is a second-image way of describing the location of fear. Either of these explanations follows from a reading of Waltz's *Man, the State, and War*.

In *Theory of International Politics*, Waltz no longer relies on his first and second images to supplement war. He suggests that anarchy itself is the location of fear. The structure of anarchy means states must compete for power in order to survive in this self-help system. The security dilemma is an attribute of international anarchy, according to Waltz. Because security questions can never be finally resolved in a situation of structural anarchy, competition is unavoidable and conflict is likely. So, on this third image reading of *Lord of the Flies*, the boys end up in deadly conflict with one another because fear is located in the insecurity of international anarchy itself.

While each of these locations of fear at first seems to make a lot of sense, none of them can be persuasively upheld when we remember that prior to the introduction of the beast – the representation in the film of fear – the boys got on well (see Box 2.2). They did not at all seem like boys behaving badly because they were evil by nature, so the film fails to make the case that fear is located in the first image. Nor do they organize themselves badly before they believe in the beast, into competitive and increasingly conflictual groups. So a second-image explanation of fear is also discredited. It is only after most of the boys embrace the fear of the beast that conflict occurs within anarchy. Anarchy itself, then, is never the location of fear. Anarchy does not create the fear that Waltz theorizes in *Theory of International Politics*. Rather, *fear creates the effects that Waltz attributes to anarchy – prioritizing survival, self-help over cooperation, and either conflict or competitive balancing.* According to the film, then, the source of fear is not internal to any of the three images – individuals, internal social and political organizations, or anarchy. So where is fear located?

To think about this question, let's reexamine Simon's declaration that the beast may be 'only us'. Simon is the one boy who knows the 'truth' about the beast – that there is no beast, that the beast is but a dead paratrooper, and that the boys have nothing to fear except (as the old saying goes) fear itself. Simon recognizes that the boys are afraid, and he recognizes that the boys are probably just scaring one another. The boys in various ways invent the beast – by land, then by sea, and then by air – as something to fear. But the fear isn't a fear of human nature or bad social and political organizations or international anarchy. The fear is the fear of fear itself. By inventing this fear among themselves and then deploying it against themselves, the boys bring about all the effects of international anarchy that Waltz predicts in his two books. But, crucially, before the boys embrace and deploy this fear, none of Waltz's predictions about international anarchy are actualized.

Fear, then, is the final supplement to Waltz's theory. It is not a first-image problem. It is not a second-image problem. And it is not (as so many IR theorists have been persuaded to believe) a third-image problem systematically built into the structure of international anarchy. *Fear is what is always missing from Waltz's theory.* But without adding fear none of the competitive and potentially conflictual things he predicts will occur in a system of structural anarchy. Put differently, the ways in which Waltz deploys the myth 'international anarchy is the permissive cause of war' make no sense without his theories being supplemented by fear, a fear that is *not* a necessary attribute of any of his three images (see Table 2.6).

Since this is the case, then it is important to look at how fear is characterized by Waltz. Waltz characterizes fear is as something that always divides people, states, societies, and worlds. Even if fear leads to balancing among states (something that could not be illustrated in the film because Ralph's group never has the power to compete with Jack's group), this balancing is never a cooperative endeavour. It is

Table 2.6 The locations of fear in *Lord of the Flies*

Location	Description	Illustration
First image	Human nature	Jack and his followers' increasing savagery
Second image	International organization of states and societies	Jack's bad tribe against Ralph's good tribe
Third image	International anarchy	Competitive, self-help system in which boys create security dilemma on island
None of Waltz's images	Irrationally generated by the boys themselves and externalized	The beast

always the result of fear. But there is absolutely *nothing* in either of Waltz's books that ever makes the case for theorizing fear in this way. Fear simply is assumed to be divisive.

What if fear functioned differently? What if fear united people for good rather than divided them for evil (or even benign) competition? International anarchy would not look the same. Anarchy would means something very different in IR theory. Anarchy, however much it was supplemented by fear, would not be a permissive cause of war because war would not be the likely outcome of a fear that united people around a good cause.

It is this fear, functioning for cooperative ends, that we find in the neoidealist myth about international anarchy. This is the myth we will explore in Chapter 3.

Suggestions for further thinking

Topic 1 Neorealism

Waltz's *Theory of International Politics* is widely regarded as the book that laid the theoretical foundation for the IR tradition of neorealism. There is an abundance of commentary on this subject. Some classic statements include Robert O. Keohane's 1986 edited volume *Neorealism and its Critics*. This book reproduces several chapters from *Theory of International Politics* and includes a wide array of criticisms of Waltz's work, from institutionalist to critical theory to postmodern perspectives. More recently, Barry Buzan, Charles Jones, and Richard Little collaborated on a book that is not so much a critique of Waltz's work as it is a critical extension of it. The authors make the case for a selective Waltzian neorealism, one that both drops some of Waltz's ideas and supplements them with their own. What is missing from these traditional critiques of neorealism are any sustained gender analyses of Waltz's work. Christine Sylvester's book *Feminist Theory and International Relations in a Postmodern Era* and chapter 2 in J. Ann Tickner's *Gender and International Relations* correct this oversight.

Suggested reading

Robert O. Keohane (ed.) (1986) *Neorealism and its Critics*. New York: Columbia University Press.

Barry Buzan, Charles Jones, and Richard Little (1993) *The Logic of Anarchy: Neorealism to Structural Realism*. New York: Columbia University Press.

Christine Sylvester (1994) *Feminist Theory and International Relations in a Postmodern Era*. Cambridge: Cambridge University Press, especially Chapter 3.

J. Ann Tickner (1992) *Gender in International Relations: Feminist Perspectives on Achieving Global Security*. New York: Columbia University Press, especially Chapter 2.

Topic 2 The uses of fear in IR theory

Richard Ashley's 1989 engagement with Waltzian neorealism argues not only that 'statecraft is mancraft' but that fear is a vital supplement to Waltz's theory of international anarchy. Many of the themes initially expressed by Ashley are picked up on and applied more generally by David Campbell in his work on international security.

Suggested reading

Richard K. Ashley (1989) 'Living on Borderlines: Man, Poststructuralism, and War', in James Der Derian and Michael Shapiro (eds) *International/Intertextual Relations: Postmodern Readings of World Politics*. Lexington, Mass.: Lexington Books, pp. 259–321.

David Campbell (1992) *Writing Security*. Minneapolis: University of Minnesota Press.

Note on the American film of Lord of the Flies

If you can't find the British film version of *Lord of the Flies*, it is best to read William Golding's novel (which is worth reading anyway) rather than to turn to the 1994 American film version directed by Harry Hook. The American version makes many critical deviations from Golding's book that change the motivations for the boys' actions on the island and (most importantly for our purposes) that change the function of fear. First, the boys in the American version are all from the same American military academy. They already know one another, they have a pre-established social hierarchy and rigid military hierarchy, and they bring values like the importance of conflict and survival to the island rather than develop them on the island because of their changed circumstances. Second, a wounded adult (Captain Benson) survives the plane crash. His presence and his possible recovery mean that hierarchy may be guaranteed by an adult. This doesn't happen because (bizarrely) Captain Benson rushes off in the middle of the night in a feverish state to take refuge in a cave. Some of the boys think he has died. But, as Simon discovers, it is Captain Benson who is 'the monster'. Finally and most importantly, fear is not the motivation for the breakdown of the boys' hierarchy and their entering into a savage anarchy. Jack leaves the group when Ralph criticizes him for letting the fire burn out. This is well before there is widespread fear of 'the monster'.

Idealism

Is there an international society?

If the myth 'anarchy is the permissive cause of war' suggests that conflict is an inevitable aspect of international affairs so long as anarchy prevails, then the myth 'there is an international society' offers some hope that the conflictual aspects of international anarchy – and possibly international anarchy itself – can be overcome. According to this myth, transforming international politics so that it becomes cooperative rather than conflictual does not necessitate moving from anarchy to hierarchy – from an international system without an orderer to an international system with an orderer. Instead, all it requires is mediating or replacing anarchy with community. In other words, world government may not be the only way out of anarchy. International community – a formal or informal collective and cooperative set of social relationships among sovereign nation-states – may be an alternative to world government *and* an alternative to international anarchy.

This way of thinking about international community is most commonly associated with the IR tradition of idealism (a subset of the larger tradition of liberalism). Idealists believe that there is a basic goodness to people that can be corrupted by bad forms of organization. These bad types of organizations are found at the level of the state and society. It is these bad forms of organizations that divide people and lead to misunderstandings among them (see Table 3.1). If people could only be organized in ways that allow them to really, truly, and honestly communicate with one another, then they could see what they have in common and unite around common standards of goodness, truth, beauty, and justice. Or (somewhat less optimistically) they could at least put into place rules and laws to temper conflict and facilitate cooperation. Either way, good organizations can lead to good changes in people, all of whom are basically good – have a good moral core – even if they occasionally behave badly. And good forms of organization are possible not only domestically but internationally because even international social relations are marked much more by harmony (when there is pure communication) than by conflict.

Idealism is arguably the founding tradition of IR theory (Walker, 1993). Even so, its influence over IR scholars and practitioners has waned over the years. Idealism is seen to have failed to 'make the world safe for democracy' as President Woodrow Wilson claimed it could during WWI, even when its principles were institutionalized into international organizations like the League of Nations and later the United Nations. Realism won most of the important intellectual debates during WWII and the Cold War. And when its usefulness was threatening to fade away, Kenneth Waltz reinvented it as neorealism in his *Theory of International Politics*, thereby providing IR theorists with a seemingly timeless account of the behaviour of actors in a situation of structural anarchy (see Chapter 2).

Table 3.1   Idealism

Actors	Nature of actors
Humans	All morally good
States and societies	Good – if organized through *pure* communication Bad – if organized through *impure* communication

But as the Cold War thawed during the later half of the 1980s and the Berlin Wall came down in 1989, Waltz's timeless truths about competition, conflict, and balancing in a system of structural anarchy no longer rang true. The East–West rivalry was over, arms control agreements seemed to proliferate faster than armaments, democracy spread internationally, and human rights and humanitarian intervention were given practical and not just rhetorical emphasis by many sovereign nation-states. These were not outcomes Waltz or any other realist or neorealist anarchy theorist would have predicted. Sure, if international anarchy had been replaced by international hierarchy – by a world government – then maybe these cooperative practices could be accounted for. But international anarchy as realists and neorealists defined it persisted in the aftermath of the Cold War, and neither realist nor neorealist scholars could satisfactorily explain the cooperative behaviour they observed, especially in the realm of international security.

But while realist and neorealist scholars where stunned by some post-Cold War developments, neoidealist and (more broadly) neoliberal scholars were not. The basic international harmony of social and/or economic relations seemed to them to explain why we were suddenly experiencing a more cooperative international environment. One neoidealist scholar in particular – Charles Kegley – made the argument that the post-Cold War world looked very much like the world Woodrow Wilson envisioned decades before. Kegley first made this argument in his 1993 article 'The Neoidealist Moment in International Studies? Realist Myths and the New International Realities'. He later clarified and crystallized it in his essay 'The Neoliberal Challenge to Realist Theories of World Politics: An Introduction' (1995).

In this chapter I will explore how in both essays Kegley utilizes the myth 'there is an international society' by 're-envisioning' Woodrow Wilson's classical idealist outlook for the post-Cold War era (Debrix, 1999). The myth that 'there is an international society' presumably functions through a domestic analogy – by drawing a parallel between what happens within states in their domestic relations to what happens among states in their international relations. For Kegley, this means that social relations and proper societies do not stop at the borders of sovereign nation-states. If we can have social spaces within states, there is nothing to prevent us from also having social spaces among states. I will elaborate on Kegley's use of the myth 'there is an international society' by summarizing what Kegley's essays say, relating that to the myth 'there is an international society', and reconsidering the myth function of Kegley's arguments about post-Cold War international politics through the film *Independence Day*.

Set in a post-Cold War world, *Independence Day* comically and upliftingly tells the story of an alien invasion of the earth – an invasion which has the effect of uniting humanity against the common enemy of the alien invaders. It demonstrates that, even in the absence of an orderer – in an anarchical world – states can set aside their differences, unite for the greater good, and overcome international anarchy. As such, it illustrates many of the basic tenets of neoidealism that Kegley claims epitomize this post-Cold War world. Yet in telling this story, the film raises the question 'Is there anything "international" about Kegley's "international society" or is it just an extension of one state's domestic society?' If the answer is it is just an extension of one state's domestic society, then Kegley's supposed domestic analogy does not draw a parallel between a domestic and an international space. Rather than a domestic analogy, it is simply a domestication of international space. In other words, *Independence Day* suggests that the supposed post-Cold War 'international society' may just be an enlarged domestic society. And if that is the case, then there is not necessarily an international society because there is nothing collective or collaborative about one state domesticating international space.

What does the myth say?

The most striking thing about Kegley's two essays is that they never make an argument for the myth 'there is an international society'. International society is simply assumed to exist. Its existence needs no defending. Arguments in defence of an international society simply go without saying. But if Kegley makes no argument for an international society and only mentions international society in passing in his essays, what make his texts appropriate for illustrating this myth? The answer is that without assuming that an international society exists, the rest of Kegley's arguments make no sense. In other words, the existence of an international society is vital to Kegley's explanation of cooperation in a post-Cold War world.

Kegley's essays tell the story of post-Cold War cooperation not by focusing on the myth 'there is an international society' but by focusing on the duelling traditions of realism and idealism. He acknowledges that during the Cold War, realist principles seemed to make sense. They explained things like 'the lust for power, appetite for imperial expansion, struggle for hegemony, a superpower arms race, and obsession with national security' that marked 'the conflict-ridden fifty-year system between 1939 and 1989' (Kegley, 1993:133; 1995:6). But then the Cold War ended. It was 'the end of the world as we know it'.

This lead Kegley to wonder 'whether it is time to revise, reconstruct, or, more boldly, reject orthodox realism' (Kegley, 1995:3; 1993:134). His answer is yes, for two reasons. One is that orthodox realism is at best incomplete because it cannot satisfactorily explain post-Cold War cooperation among states (Kegley, 1993:134–5; 1995:5–9; see Table 3.2). The other reason is that there is an existing tradition of international theory that better explains this cooperation, and this is an idealism or liberalism that has its roots in the ideas of Woodrow Wilson.

Table 3.2 What can realism explain and what can realism not explain?

Realism can explain	Realism cannot explain
Cold War conflictual activities among sovereign nation-states, e.g.:	Post-Cold War realities of cooperation among sovereign nation-states, e.g.:
'lust for power'	'march of democracy'
'appetite for imperial expansion'	'increase in liberal free trade agreements'
'struggle for hegemony'	'renewed role of the United Nations'
'superpower arms race'	'proliferation of arms control agreements'
'obsession with national security'	'international humanitarianism'

Source: Kegley, 1993

Kegley argues that the idealist worldview can be summed up in the following core principles:

1. Human nature is essentially 'good' or altruistic, and people are therefore capable of mutual aid and collaboration.
2. The fundamental human concern for the welfare of others makes progress possible (that is, the Enlightenment's faith in the possibility of improving civilization is reaffirmed).
3. Bad human behavior is the product not of evil people but of evil institutions and structural arrangements that motivate people to act selfishly and to harm others – including making war.
4. War is not inevitable and its frequency can be reduced by eradicating the anarchical conditions that encourage it.
5. War and injustice are international problems that require collective or multilateral rather than national efforts to eliminate them.
6. International society must reorganize itself institutionally to eliminate the anarchy that makes problems such as war likely.

(Kegley, 1995:4)

Read together, these six principles illustrate a movement in idealist theorizing from the individual level to the state level to the international level. They begin by focusing on theories of human nature, then try to account for human behaviour not because of human nature but because of their institutional and structural arrangements (how they are organized), finally concluding that international society can be rearranged so that bad behaviour (this time of states as well as of individuals) can be lessened if not eliminated. These are the very same three levels of analysis that Waltz identified in his book *Man, the State, and War*. But Waltz and someone like Kegley have very different ways of thinking about these three images. Most importantly for our purposes is how they think about the third image, the international level.

For Waltz, the international level is where anarchy is located. And because Waltz argues that anarchy is the permissive cause of war, then the international level is where war is located. In contrast, for Kegley, the international level is not where war is located. Violence and war are never finally located in any of the three images for Kegley. This is because war and conflict – bad behaviour – can be illuminated if only political and social arrangements are better organized. In the place of anarchy at the international level, Kegley is keen to substitute 'international society'. If organized properly, international society can 'eliminate the anarchy that makes problems such as war possible' (Kegley, 1995:4) (see Table 3.3).

This is precisely what Kegley implies is occurring in a post-Cold War era. He cites 'the march of democracy' within states around the globe, increases in liberal free-trade arrangements that assume trust and the benefit of all, strengthening of international law, the renewed role of international institutions like the United Nations to undertake collective security initiatives, the proliferation of arms control agreements, and international humanitarian responses to state human-rights violations as evidence of the fulfilment of Wilson's specific idealist predictions about what international politics would look like (Kegley, 1993:135–8; 1995:10–14).

Table 3.3 How do Waltz and Kegley differently characterize international politics?

Waltz	Kegley
International politics is anarchical, and anarchy is the permissive cause of war. Therefore, war and conflict are ultimately located at the international level and cannot be eliminated because anarchy cannot be eliminated.	International politics can be reorganized around international society rather than international anarchy, potentially eliminating problems like war and conflict without replacing international anarchy with international hierarchy (world government)

And, so, to the six core principles that Woodrow Wilson embraced, Kegley offers a seventh, post-Cold War, neoidealist principle:

> This goal [of reorganizing international society so that it can eliminate the anarchy that makes problems such as war likely] is realistic because history suggests that global change and cooperation are not only possible but empirically pervasive.
>
> (Kegley, 1995:4; my brackets)

These post-Cold War developments are vitally important to Kegley. They seem to empirically demonstrate that neoidealism is a theory that describes things as they really are in the post-Cold War era, something idealism failed to do for its historical era. Even more importantly, they demonstrate that 'the motives that animate the goals of state are not immutable. They *can* change' (Kegley, 1993:135–7;1995:11; italics in the original). Conflict is not an inevitability in international life.

Kegley's point is not to dispute that the Cold War was an era marked by conflict and the disposition of the Eastern and Western blocs to go to war with one another. That happened. He accepts that. But, he argues, now that the Cold War is over, states are behaving cooperatively. That means they changed from being conflictual with one another to being cooperative with one another. And, given the history of superpower conflict during the Cold War, this change is a very big one.

Why has the behaviour of sovereign nation-states in a post-Cold War era become so cooperative? Before answering this question, let's just remind ourselves that the answer is *not* because the international system changed from being anarchical to hierarchical. The answer is *not* that during the Cold War there was no world government and in the post-Cold War era there is a world government. There is still no world government. Waltz believed that cooperation around security issues could occur if anarchy gave way to hierarchy. How does Kegley explain post-Cold War cooperation in the absence of hierarchy – in the absences of an orderer?

Part of Kegley's answer is that these changes from conflictual to cooperative behaviour among states follow from a change in the international organization of states. The Cold War bipolar world system of two opposed blocs locked into a deadly battle with one another has given way to a new form of international organization, and this begins to explain why cooperation is occurring. It was the bad organization of international politics during the Cold War that kept idealist (and now neoidealist) principles of cooperation from being realized.

On this point, Kegley is not claiming that the end of the Cold War will mark the end of conflict altogether. He acknowledges, for example, that not all of Wilson's ideas make sense for the post Cold-War era. For example, Wilson did not think through all the implications and uses to which self-determination (letting people decide for themselves how and by whom they would be governed) might be put, and this has led to a lot of bloodshed within and among states in the post-Cold War era (Kegley, 1993:137). But what it does mean is that – while it will never be a perfect state of affairs – with the end of the Cold War states are now engaged in restoring 'a place for morality in foreign policy' (Kegley, 1993:138). They are pursuing collective, cooperative interests that all states have always had in common – like peace, justice, and a better way of life. These are interests about welfare within and among states rather than warfare among states. And these moral goals that lead to a better way of life for people and states are as much in states' individualistic national interests as they are in their collective interests (Kegley, 1993:142). Because the world has been reorganized, they are realizable once again.

But for idealism and neoidealism, moral progress among sovereign nation-states does not result merely from the reorganizing of relations among sovereign nation-states. If the world changed from a bipolar system to a differently organized system, this in itself would not necessarily account for increased cooperation. For even realists and neorealists like Waltz acknowledge these changes within anarchy. Something else is at work in Kegley's argument, as it was in Wilson's, that makes cooperation possible. That 'something else' is an international society. For a neoidealist like Kegley, international society is the space in which moral progress occurs. But where does this international society come from? For any brand of idealist – including Kegley – it comes from drawing a domestic analogy. If there is society within states, then there can be (and in a post-Cold War world there is) society among states.

To understand the importance of this domestic analogy to the myth 'there is an international society', let's explore two aspects of it. First, how does a domestic society serve as a space in which moral progress can occur? Second, how is this society 'transferred' from the domestic or state level to the international level?

For a neoidealist, the sovereign nation-state is not just a political space. It is also a social space. Indeed, government is the formal institutional expression of social relations within a state. If the state is organized in a good way, then it can organize its domestic social relations so that moral progress can occur within it. What is a good form of state organization for a neoidealist, and how can this good form of state organization enable moral progress in its domestic society? For a neoidealist, the best form of governmental organization is democracy.

Democracy is the best form of organization because it is the least restrictive. It is the least repressive. It is the form of governance that most encourages freedom of expression. Democracy is government by the people. So the voice of any democratic sovereign nation-state is really the collective voice of its people. This is important because, as all idealists believe, people are basically good. If they are free to express their goodness within their state, then this goodness moves up from the individual level (good people) to the state level (good state). Furthermore, good people within a democratic state have a good influence on others within that state – those citizens who are behaving badly. Moral progress occurs within democratic

Figure 3.1 Democratically organized state and society

sovereign nation-states, then, because this good form of political and social organization means that citizens behaving well 'enlighten' citizens behaving badly. Selfishness diminishes, as does the motivation to do harm to one's fellow citizens, so long as people are free to express their internal goodness. And this purity of communication is something that the democratic state ensures (Figure 3.1).

Of course, not all sovereign nation-states are democratic. Some of them are organized autocratically – with state authority flowing from unenlightened governmental elites on to its repressed people. Neoidealists believe that it is these sorts of autocratic governments that cause conflict in international politics. They are the ones that don't work for the collective good because they don't really know what the collective good is, as they are unenlightened by their good people. They tell their citizens what to do rather than listening to them and representing their moral interests (Figure 3.2). If only these autocratic sovereign nation-states could be reorganized internally to become democratic, then the good people within them could enlighten their wayward leaders. This is why Woodrow Wilson wanted to 'make the world safe for democracy'.

This answers the question 'how does a domestic society serve as a space in which moral progress can occur?' What about the second question – how is this society 'transferred' from the domestic or state level to the international level?

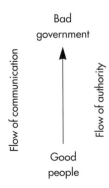

Figure 3.2 Autocratically organized state and society

Neoidealists offer two answers to this second question. The classic answer – Wilson's answer – is that by 'making the world safe for democracy', democratic states will have an influence on autocratic states (either through benevolent enlightenment or though fighting just wars against bad governments to liberate their good people), transforming them into democratic states, and we will end up with an international society of democratic states. If democracy is a form of governance that expresses the will of the people and if all states are democratic, then the individual 'domestic societies' within states become one big collective 'international society' among states (Figure 3.3).

Kegley accepts this answer and adds to it. He is excited about the international 'march of democracy' in a post-Cold War era in part because democracies almost never wage war against each other (Kegley, 1995:10). All this proves Wilson's point that democratic states develop international social relationships among themselves that are cooperative rather than conflictual.

In addition to this, though, Kegley stresses the influence of cross-border communication in connecting people within domestic spaces and lessening the separations among peoples. As Kegley puts it, 'People matter . . . public sentiment is captured instantaneously in our age of global communications knit together by cables, the airwaves, and the fax machine. The distinction between domestic and foreign affairs has broken down. . . . This also follows Wilson's belief that lowering barriers between countries would be a barrier to warfare' (Kegley, 1995:11).

With all this communication among good people, domestic differences are giving way to common interests. Because the goodness of people is communicated, warfare (which is an outgrowth of an inability to communicate the goodness of people) is on the decline. In this international society – a society composed of states but also primarily of the people within states – moral progress is occurring, as people de-emphasize warfare and reemphasize welfare (Figure 3.4).

This is how Kegley transfers social relations that occur within states to social relations that occur among states. By analogy to domestic society, 'there is an

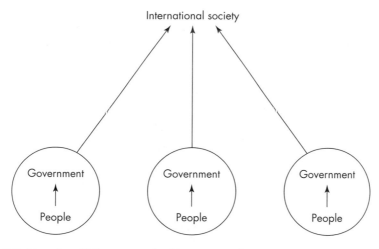

Figure 3.3 How does Wilson enact the 'domestic analogy'?

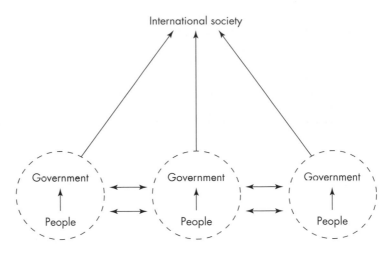

Figure 3.4 How does Kegley enact the 'domestic analogy'?

international society'. It is this international society that, for Kegley, explains cooperation in the post-Cold War era. And it is Kegley's myth of post-Cold War international society that is explored in the film *Independence Day*.

Independence Day

The opening sequence of *Independence Day* sets the stage for an action/adventure story in which moral good triumphs over irredeemable evil. The camera's first image is of the US flag flying on the moon. From the flag, the camera takes us to a plaque left by US astronauts, inscribed with the words 'We came in peace for all mankind.' The camera slowly zooms in on the word 'peace'. Then the moon trembles. A shadow passes over it. We follow the shadow to the edge of the moon until a shot of the earth appears in centre frame. Entering our frame from the top is an alien spacecraft. It is the spacecraft that is casting this long shadow over the moon. Cut to white. Cut to an exterior of the Research for Extraterrestrial Intelligence Institute in New Mexico. Cut to interior shot. A young man is practising his putting inside the listening station. Hi-tech equipment fills the room. The man hears a signal that we know and he suspects is being emitted by aliens. In the background, we hear REM singing 'It's the end of the world as we know it, and I feel fine'. This action takes place on 2 July.

This opening sequence tells us a lot about the world of *Independence Day* and the struggles to come. The elements that the film will use to make sense of the world – humans vs. aliens, peace vs. conflict, and purity of communication vs. corrupted communication – are all evident in this sequence. *Independence Day* is not only a comically styled remake of an outer-space B film, it is also the perfect script for telling Kegley's neoidealist tale of international cooperation in a post-Cold War era. And, most importantly for our purposes, the film offers us clues – even in this opening sequence – as to how to functionally rethink the myth 'there is an international society'.

On the heels of this opening sequence, *Independence Day* introduces us to an ensemble cast and their various interlinking storylines. The film gives us not one hero, but at least four (all of whom happen to be male) and possibly many more (including some women). The four central heroes are President Bill Whitmore, David, Steve, and Russell. President Whitmore is a veteran fighter pilot from the Gulf War. He is young. He is liberal. And he is moral. His morality is testified to by his wife who reminds the president that he is a bad liar. 'Stick to the truth,' she tells him. 'That's what you're good at.' President Whitmore represents the incorruptibility of communication. He cannot tell a lie – or, really, he cannot tell a lie and get away with it. It is President Whitmore who will take the lead in organizing the world's response to the alien invasion.

We find our next hero, David, playing chess with his ageing father in New York's Central Park. David is a good son, and he was a good husband. Part of his story is that he has been divorced from the president's assistant, Connie, for four years but he still honors his commitment to their marriage. A sign of this is that he still wears his wedding ring. David works as a computer troubleshooter for a satellite television company. He is also a committed environmentalist who, for example, rides a bike rather than drives a car and makes sure his colleagues are recycling their rubbish.

It is David who, in trying to restore uninterrupted service to his TV station's customers, discovers the alien signal hidden in the US satellites. At first, he is comforted by the discovery that the signal is reducing itself and will disappear in seven hours. But when he sees the alien spacecraft – now broken up into pieces

Plate 3.1 Honest-faced US President Bill Whitmore.
© Twentieth Century Fox
Source: http://www.movieweb.com/movie/id4

assembled over the world's major cities – he realizes that the signal he has found is an alien countdown to the destruction of humankind. He explains how the signal works in a conversation with his boss.

David: It's like chess. First you strategically position your pieces. Then when the timing's right you strike. See. They're positioning themselves all over the world using this one signal to synchronize their efforts. Then, in approximately 6 hours, the signal's gonna disappear and the countdown's gonna be over.
Boss: And then what?
David: Checkmate.

David goes to Washington, D.C., so he can warn his ex-wife and the president. David is a morally good man who understands the technical workings of impure/alien communication. It becomes his task to disable this corrupted alien communication. He does so by planting a virus in the alien computer, thereby disabling the forcefields around their ships that have protected the aliens from attack.

Our next hero Steve, a pilot in the US military who dreams of flying the space-shuttle for NASA, flies himself and David in an alien craft into the belly of the alien mothership where David plants his virus and thereby disables the defensive shields. Steve is our man of courage and adventure who actively unites goodness of purpose (the president's agenda) with technical know-how (David's plan to plant the virus).

While Steve (like President Whitmore) is our legitimate military hero, our final hero, Russell, is anything but legitimate. He is a drunken cropduster who fought in the 'wrong war' – Vietnam. And he is a local laughing stock because he insists that ten years earlier he was abducted by aliens. But Russell redeems himself when, fighting in the alien counteroffensive, he flies his plane with an undetectable live bomb into the body of the alien ship, destroying it. Russell, then, was always a good man who spoke the truth. He was just misunderstood. (See Table 3.4.)

As this plot and presentation of characters demonstrate, *Independence Day* makes sense of the world by closely following a neoidealist script. What is typical of this world is that it is inhabited by morally good humans who, when properly understood through good communication, are able to lead good, moral, peaceful lives. The humans we are introduced to are all US citizens. Part of their ability to express their goodness, the film hints, is because they are organized in a moral way, in a democratic sovereign nation-state. So, like neoidealism, the film makes sense of the world by assuming that good people do good things in good organizations. This is also what is typical of the world (Box 3.1).

But then, just as in the aftermath of the Cold War, the world as we know it ends. In the historical Cold War script, evil (represented in the US view by the communist threat) is 'defeated'. But in the cinematic post-Cold War, post-communist script of *Independence Day*, a new evil is introduced. This new evil is the aliens.

The aliens are not initially treated as if they are evil. Because the moral goodness of human beings is assumed by neoidealism and by the characters in the film, it is not surprising that the film begins by extending this presumption of moral goodness to the aliens. Early on, the president addresses the nation, saying 'The question of whether or not we are alone in the universe has been answered. Although it's understandable that many of us feel a sense of hesitation or even fear, we must

Table 3.4 The heroes in *Independence Day*

Hero	What makes him heroic
US President Bill Whitmore	This president cannot tell a lie and therefore symbolizes the incorruptibility of communication. As such, he is able to conceive of a morally just plan to beat the aliens and to mobilize a moral society through pure communication.
David, the computer troubleshooter for a satellite TV company	He is a morally good man who understands the technical workings of impure/alien communication well enough to disable them. He does this by planting a virus in the alien computer.
Steve, the US military fighter pilot	A man of courage and adventure who actively unites goodness of purpose (the president's agenda) with technical know-how (David's plan to plant the virus) by flying an alien craft into the mothership
Russell, the Vietnam veteran, now a drunken cropduster, who claims to have been abducted by aliens	Russell sacrifices himself for his children and the rest of humanity by carrying out a suicide mission that destroys an alien ship. He proves he is a good man who was always speaking the truth but who was just misunderstood.

Box 3.1 What is typical in the world of *Independence Day*?

- Good people do good deeds in good organizations
- Bad things follow from impaired communication
- Human beings are morally progressive

---

attempt to reserve judgment.' 'To reserve judgment' here means to not assume the worst about the aliens but to assume the best about them until there is clear evidence to the contrary. Throughout, he resists the advice of the secretary of defense to attack the alien craft.

Steve echoes this sentiment when he tells his girlfriend Jasmine, 'I really don't believe they (the aliens) flew over 90 billion light years to come down here and start a fight, to get rowdy.' These views are widespread throughout the government and among the public. Keeping in mind that firing guns into the air can be a sign of celebration in Los Angeles, a local newscaster tells his audience, 'Once again the LAPD is asking Los Angelinos not to fire their guns at the visitor spacecraft. You may inadvertently trigger an inner-stellar war.' And throughout the US at least, some groups of people gather to 'party' with the aliens.

Because the aliens are assumed to be good by nature, the president authorizes an attempt to communicate with them – to express to the aliens that the earthlings mean them no harm. Communication itself is believed to be pure. Indeed, it is the president, as we know, who symbolizes the incorruptibility of communication. Not knowing how to communicate with the aliens, the government sends up 'Welcome Wagon' – a military plane with enormous light panels – to greet the alien ship. The aliens fire on and destroy 'Welcome Wagon', just as the president learns from David that the alien signal is a countdown to an alien attack. The president's bad decision to send up 'Welcome Wagon' comes from having incomplete information. Communication was impaired, and bad things followed from that. The aliens proceed to destroy many major cities worldwide. The president and others (including David) flee on Air Force One. July 2 comes to a close.

Even in the face of all of this alien destruction of the earth, in the president's mind lingers the hope that the aliens' bad behaviour is not attributable to their being evil creatures. Yes, the president orders a counterattack against the aliens on 3 July, one that is justified even from a neoidealist point of view because it is defensive. Yet even when this counterattack with conventional weapons fails miserably, the president is still not persuaded by the secretary of defense to use nuclear weapons against the aliens. For while it is acceptable from a neoidealist perspective to defend oneself in the face of aggression, it is not alright to attempt to annihilate a species that could be morally progressive. The president must know for sure if the aliens are morally good or bad. He gets his answer when Steve brings a live alien to Area 51, where the president and his entourage have assembled.

Plate 3.2 The aliens destroy Washington, D.C., and cities around the world.
© Twentieth Century Fox
Source: http://www.movieweb.com/movie/id4

An Area 51 scientist explains to the president that the aliens are very much like humans. Their bodies are frail like human bodies. But they lack vocal cords. They communicate through telepathy, through extra-sensory perception. As a group of scientists are examining the live alien Steve has brought in, the alien 'captures' one of them by first capturing his mind. It does this by looking into the scientist's eyes. It then manipulates the scientist's vocal cords to speak to the president and other onlookers.

Alien: Release me. Release me.
President: I know there is much we can learn from each another if we can negotiate a truce. We can find a way to co-exist. Can there be a peace between us?
Alien: Peace. No peace.
President: What is it you want us to do?
Alien: Die. Die.

Then the alien links up telepathically with the president. Military personnel shoot the alien, wounding it enough for it to release the tormented president. The president speaks again.

President: I saw his thoughts. I saw what they're planning to do. They're like locusts. They're moving from planet to planet, their whole civilization. After they've consumed every natural resource, they move on. And we're next.

A soldier shoots and kills the alien.

President: Nuke 'em. Let's nuke the bastards.

The president's decision to 'nuke the bastards' may seem to veer from the neoidealist script into a more realist or neorealist one. Conflict marks the relationship between the humans and the aliens. The aliens want to annihilate the humans, and now the president wants to annihilate the aliens. Can this ever be justified in a neoidealist world?

The answer is yes because the aliens are beyond the moral boundary of goodness and cannot be morally recuperated. It would not have been neoidealist for the president to just assume the aliens were bastards and to nuke them earlier, as the very realist secretary of defense advised him to do. But with all barriers to pure communication between the president and the alien removed through telepathy, the president knows for sure that the aliens are not morally progressive. They will not negotiate. They have done this before, to other species on other planets. The aliens are morally bad. They deserve to die. Defending the human species is a just cause. So is annihilating a morally unprogressive species. None of this contradicts the neoidealist principle that humans are morally good. For, as the president learns, there is nothing *morally* human about the aliens. And that is what matters to a neoidealist. The aliens, then, do not represent a departure from the neoidealist story. Rather, they represent what is deviant in a neoidealist world (Box 3.2).

But the nuclear option fails. The US military is unable to defeat the aliens. It is at this point that a new strategy is devised. And, of course, it is now 4 July.

Box 3.2 What is deviant in the world of *Independence Day*?

- Bad aliens do bad deeds *not* because they are badly organized but because their communication is impaired and because they are morally corrupt
- Alien communication is corrupted and corrupting
- Aliens are not morally progressive

First, David's idea to plant a virus in the alien computer – to corrupt corrupted communication – is embraced by the president. If successful, David's plan will mean that the defensive shields around the alien ships will be dismantled for about 30 seconds. If a counteroffensive were launched during that time, it would have a fair chance of success. Second, the president decides to coordinate such a counter-offensive worldwide. When the secretary of defense protests against this plan, the president fires him. The secretary of defense represents not only realism but also distorted and secretive human communication. For example, he kept secret from the president that years ago aliens really did land at Area 51, as rumours had long suggested. His dismissal removes another barrier to a neoidealist success.

Plate 3.3 Steve and David team up to fly an old alien ship into the alien mothership where they plant a virus that disables the ships' protective shields.
© Twentieth Century Fox
Source: http://www.movieweb.com/movie/id4

But there is a problem. How can a worldwide counterattack be coordinated? Earthly satellites are ineffective forms of communication because alien ships interfere with them. And, even if they could be used, since the aliens have already used them against the earthlings, any message sent by satellite would surely be intercepted. The US military ends up spreading the word of its counterattack using the purest, most basic, and most universal of all military languages – Morse code.

Steve successfully flies the alien craft into the mothership. David successfully plants the virus in the mothership's computer, thereby disabling the alien defences. Russell has his sacrificial and redemptive moment of glory when he penetrates the alien ship and blows it up. And, as word of this success is transmitted via Morse code around the world, earthly successes increase against the alien ships.

The message of *Independence Day*, then, is that international cooperation for a just cause leads to peace. Pure communication among humankind enables states to unite around such a just cause. And this just cause can be communicated, embraced, and implemented because 'there is an international society'. Or is there?

Fear and leadership in *Independence Day*

On this first reading, *Independence Day* seems to support all of the core principles of neoidealism, leading to a domestic analogy that draws a parallel between domestic society and international society. The film supports the idea that the defining characteristic of humans is that they are morally good. And, to illustrate this point, human kindness abounds in *Independence Day*. For example, when the aliens start destroying cities worldwide, there is no looting, extortion of services, or reckless living for the moment. Everyone seems to be focused on helping one another. As Jasmine roams the ruins of Los Angeles, she rescues everyone she comes across, never asking for anything in return. Never mind that resources like food, water, and gasoline have become scarce commodities. The post-apocalyptic world of *Independence Day* is a space in which people are at their moral best and behave well.

In typical neoidealist fashion, this moral goodness is not confined to personal relationships among people. Good, cooperative behaviour is observed at all levels of social interaction – the personal, the state, and the international. And, from a neoidealist standpoint, it is no surprise that the film's action begins to unfold in a democratic space – in the sovereign nation-state of the US. The implication here is that all this moral behaviour on the part of US citizens is able to be expressed because these citizens have lived in a democratically organized state and society. Would this post-Cold War plot have been different if the action unfolded in the former Yugoslavia? We can only imagine that it would be. So much of the cooperative action we see in the film is attributable to good people organized into good states and good societies.

It is not a stretch, then, in either the film's script or the script of neoidealism to invoke the domestic analogy. Because there are moral people organized into good (democratic) states and societies, then there can be an international society. For Woodrow Wilson, all that is required for this hope and belief to be realized is for the world to be made safe for democracy – for all sovereign nation-states to be transformed into democratic sovereign nation-states. This isn't the plot of *Independence*

Plate 3.4 Jasmine and her son wander round Los Angeles in the aftermath of the alien invasion, rescuing survivors.
© Twentieth Century Fox
Source: http://www.movieweb.com/movie/id4

Day. But Kegley's way of moving from domestic society to international society is not only in the plot. It is the key to the human victory over the evil aliens. Kegley's move is to argue that domestic society becomes 'internationalized' though increased cross-border communications, which are assumed to be good and pure. And what does *Independence Day* give us but the purest form of cross-border communication available to militaries around the world – Morse code. Morse code unites the sovereign nation-states around the world into one just military mission against the evil aliens. The world is now safe from the aliens. 'There is an international society.'

Importantly, all of this cooperation in the post-Cold War era happens in the scripts of *Independence Day* and neoidealism *not* because the post-Cold War world has been transformed from anarchy to hierarchy – from the absence of an orderer to a world government. International cooperation is the outcome of the coordination of moral efforts by an international society. It is international society that mediates international anarchy in a neoidealist reading of *Independence Day*. It is international society that even promises to take us out of and keep us out of anarchy altogether.

Independence Day supports many of these neoidealist core ideals and moves, but it would be a mistake to conclude that it supports all of them. In particular, it would be wrong to conclude that the film supports the myth 'there is an international society'. For in addition to rehearsing many aspects of the neoidealist story, the film tells us what makes the myth 'there is an international society' function. It does so by adding two vital elements to the neoidealist plot – fear and US leadership.

Fear seems to play a starring role in both of our anarchy myths so far. In the myth 'anarchy is the permissive cause of war', fear functions to divide actors in a situation of structural anarchy. Fear leads to conflict. Fear is what makes that myth function. Fear helps the myth 'there is an international society' function as well, but to different effect. In this alternative anarchy myth, fear functions to unite people. It is the fear of the aliens that makes humans recognize what they have in common and draw upon this good moral core to act humanely towards one another.

Even if we accept the film's neoidealist proposition that fear brings out the best in people, we have to wonder what people – even democratically organized people – are like *without fear*. For example, what were all these good US citizens doing prior to the alien invasion? Because the film is set in the US in the present, most of us can judge for ourselves (by looking around US society or by thinking about its depictions in the worldwide media) if the good moral core of these characters might have been expressed prior to the alien invasion – the fear – that brought out the best in them. In my mind a pre-alien-invasion US is not full of such widespread benevolent behaviour, but of acts of racial prejudice, selfish economic advancement, militia bombings, and school shootings. Without the fear that unites people around the necessary goal of human survival, maybe social interactions are not quite as cooperative as the film suggests they are in the face of fear. And, of course, this raises the important questions: Now that the aliens have been defeated and the fear is gone, will there be an international society? Will people remain 'united'? These questions raise serious challenges to a neoidealist reading of *Independence Day*.

While the issue of fear makes us wonder if an international society will last in the aftermath of the defeat of the alien threat, the issue of US leadership makes us wonder if there was ever an international society at all. Think about it. Is there anything truly 'international' about the 'international society' we see in *Independence Day*? From the opening shot of the US flag waving on the moon until the end of the film in which the lightshow of alien spacecrafts falling from the sky becomes celebratory fireworks for the Fourth of July, *everything* in this film is about how US leadership saves humanity from the aliens. It isn't that the world has united around one cause and collectively decides what to do. Rather, it is the US president who makes all the key decisions for the entire planet! And, according to the script of *Independence Day*, this is precisely what the world is wanting and waiting for, as is made clear in an exchange between two British soldiers when they receive the Morse code message from the US military.

First British Soldier: It's from the Americans. They want to organize a counter-
      offensive.
Second British Soldier: It's about bloody time.

This isn't a dialogue about equal partners in an international community entering into cooperative relationships. It is a dialogue that suggests a hierarchical relationship between the US leader and the British follower. In *Independence Day*, 'international society' is never more than a *global extension of US domestic society*. This could not have been made more clear than it was in the president's speech to US pilots prior to their successful counteroffensive.

President: In less than an hour, aircraft from here will join others from around the world. And you will be launching the largest aerial battle in the history of mankind. Mankind . . . that word should have new meaning for all of us today. We can't be consumed by our petty differences anymore. We will be united in our common interest. Perhaps it's fate that today is the fourth of July. And you will once again be fighting for our freedom. Not from tyranny, oppression, or persecution but from annihilation. We're fighting for our right to live, to exist. And should we win the day, the fourth of July will no longer be known as an American holiday, but as the day the world declared in one voice, 'We will not go quietly into the night. We will not vanish without a fight. We're going to live on. We're going to survive. Today, we celebrate our Independence Day.'

In this speech, the president declares that the US is part of a wider human community – mankind. Mankind must no longer be a divided community. It must be what it really is – an international community. It must speak in 'one voice' and fight as one unit if it is going to defeat the aliens. And this is what the film suggests occurs. But there are a couple of troubling turns in the film that make us wonder if what the president 'says' is the same as what his speech and the film more generally 'do'.

One of these troubling turns, as I've already mentioned, is that it is the US president who makes all the decisions for 'mankind'. It is the US government that takes action. It is the US military that unites the state militaries of the world through the pure communication of Morse code. It is always the US government that is acting *on behalf of mankind – on behalf of the community of humans.* This may all be expected. If the US is indeed the most powerful state on earth, then it makes sense that it would have the necessary influence to coordinate global militaries. It makes sense that it would take the lead.

The problem is, however, that in taking the lead *the US confuses its leadership and the extension of its domestic influence internationally with an international society.* The president's speech, for example, suggests that the US mission is a mission for all of mankind. This is the same move we found in the opening sequence – with the US flag flying on the moon and the plaque left there by the US astronauts. It reads, 'We came in peace *for all mankind.*' It is an old habit for the US to imagine (or at least to say) that its acts are acts on behalf of the whole of humanity.

The US acting on behalf of the whole of humanity wouldn't be inconsistent with neoidealism if this US leadership was the first step towards an end to all domestic differences and towards a truly international society. But that isn't how things work out in *Independence Day.* For instead of erasing all domestic boundaries, one domestic boundary remains intact in the film. It is that of the US. Let's return to the president's speech. He declares, 'And should we win the day, the fourth of July will no longer be known as an American holiday, but as the day the world declared in one voice, "We will not go quietly into the night. We will not vanish without a fight. We're going to live on. We're going to survive. Today, we celebrate our Independence Day".' What the president is doing here is extending what is uniquely US to the whole world. That doesn't mean the US ceases to exist as a distinct political and social space. It means instead that US values, ideals – even holidays – are extended internationally (Figure 3.5).

Figure 3.5 How US leadership is extended in *Independence Day*

In *Independence Day*, there is no *international* society. There *appears to be* an international society because US domestic society is extended globally. But this extension of US leadership and US society does not meet the neoidealist terms of what an international society is – a formal or informal collective and cooperative set of social relationships among sovereign nation-states. 'Collective' means more than one state must make the decisions. 'Cooperative' means no one state is the leader and all the other states are the followers.

Independence Day encourages us to mistake its combinations of fear and US leadership for an international society that mediates (if not overcomes) international anarchy and ensures moral cooperation. But the world of *Independence Day* is *not* the world of an international society. It is a world in which the US is the leader, the world-wide hegemon. The US is the *orderer* of international life. Anarchy is not replaced by international community. In this film, anarchy is mediated or replaced by hierarchy – by the US as the orderer of international life, even though all the rhetoric that accompanies the action is neoidealist. Might the same series of moves be found in Kegley's neoidealism?

Kegley attributes post-Cold War cooperation to a reorganized international society – one in which increased cross-border communication has lead to commonly shared and expressed moral values resulting in more cooperative, moral international behaviour among states. But for Kegley's explanation of post-Cold War international cooperation to ring true, it must remain silent on the issues of the unifying effects of fear and, more importantly, on the role of US leadership. Kegley can acknowledge that the post-Cold War world may be less 'anarchical', but he cannot do this in the same way that Waltz would, by noting US global leadership and not an international society. If Kegley were to follow Waltz on this point, Kegley's neoidealism would not perform a domestic analogy between a domestic society and an international society, Kegley's neoidealism would be seen to confuse the extensions of one state's domestic society with an international society.

Yet the evidence Kegley presents for a better-organized international society in a post-Cold War world is the very same evidence others would offer to prove that the US is the undisputed post-Cold War global leader. By leaving US leadership so woefully neglected, we are left to wonder if 'there is an international society' that leads to cooperation in the post-Cold War anarchical world and maybe even replaces this anarchy or if, alternatively, post-Cold War cooperation results from the unopposed global spread of US influence. Put differently, might US post-Cold War leadership be so strong that Kegley mistakes it for an international society?

If this is the case, Kegley comes by this confusion/exclusion honestly. It is the same one Woodrow Wilson made in the aftermath of WWI – another post-conflict era in which the US emerged as a world leader (if not *the* world leader). And maybe that is what explains why Wilson's idealist programme seemed to fail and Kegley's neoidealist programme (at least in the immediate aftermath of the Cold War) seems to succeed.

Overall, though, it is only by leaving unaddressed the presumably unifying function of fear and the question of US global leadership in a post-Cold War era that Kegley's myth 'there is an international society' (and the international effects it promises) *appears* to be true.

Suggestions for further thinking

Topic 1 Cooperation under anarchy

The idealist and neoidealist stories of how international society mediates or even supercedes the effects of international anarchy are not the only IR stories about cooperation in relation to international anarchy. Other stories about the relationships between anarchy and cooperation abound. They are found in the so-called 'English School' tradition, in neorealism, and in neoliberal institutionalism.

For example, Hedley Bull's *The Anarchical Society* (1977) contributes to the anarchy/cooperation debate from the perspective of the misnamed English School (misnamed because its key figures were Welsh and Australian in addition to English and because the cornerstone of this tradition is arguably the writings of the Dutch legalist Hugo Grotius). Robert Keohane's *After Hegemony* is an important contribution from the neoliberal institutionalism position, while Stephen Krasner's edited collection *International Regimes* carries on the debate about international cooperation under anarchy by bringing together theorists from neorealist and neoliberal perspectives.

Suggested reading

Hedley Bull (1987) *The Anarchical Society*. London: Macmillian.

Robert O. Keohane (1984) *After Hegemony*. Princeton: Princeton University Press.

Stephen D. Krasner (ed.) (1983) *International Regimes*. Ithaca: Cornell University Press.

Topic 2 Alternative readings of Independence Day

Reading *Independence Day* as a neoidealist script is arguably only part of the story this film has to tell. For broader readings of the film that situate it in terms of IR theory, international history, and debates about teaching international politics, see the texts by Michael Rogin and Julie Webber.

Suggested reading

Michael Rogin (1998) *Independence Day.* London: British Film Institute.

Julie Webber (1998) 'Independence Day as a Cosmopolitan Moment: Teaching International Relations' (unpublished paper).

Media note

Tim Burton's *Mars Attacks!* counterposes the sanctimoniousness of *Independence Day* with sarcasm. Instead of tempting viewers to embrace a neoidealist script in which 'there is an international society', it shows aliens with a sense of humour playing with the language of neoidealism to hilarious (if disastrous) effect.

Classroom activity

An interesting teaching exercise would be to give a class a lecture (or reading assignment) on neoidealism. Then divide the students into two groups – with one group viewing *Independence Day* and the other *Mars Attacks!* Have each group come up with a report or short essay on what they think about the myth 'there is an international society' in the context of neoidealism based on their viewing of their specific film. Then assemble the class as a whole and have them present their views to each other. A follow-up discussion and/or lecture on the influences of cultural mediations for mythologizing IR 'truths' might offer an interesting conclusion to this teaching exercise.

Chapter 4

Constructivism:

Is anarchy what states make of it?

Our third and final anarchy myth, 'anarchy is what states make of it', proposes a way out of the dilemmas faced by IR scholars thinking about the effects of international anarchy deterministically. If the myth 'anarchy is the permissive cause of war' suggests that anarchy means international politics is likely to be conflictual, and the myth 'there is an international society' suggests that, mediated by international society, anarchy should be cooperative, then this new myth holds that the effects of international anarchy are not quite so predictable as either of the first two anarchy myths suggest. Anarchy is necessarily neither conflictual nor cooperative. There is no 'nature' to international anarchy. 'Anarchy is what states make of it.' If states behave conflictually towards one another, then it *appears* that the 'nature' of international anarchy is conflictual. If states behave cooperatively towards one another, then it *appears* that the 'nature' of international anarchy is cooperative. It is what states do that we must focus on to understand conflict and cooperation in international politics, according to this myth, rather than focusing on the supposed 'nature' of international anarchy. States determine the 'nature' of international anarchy. And, most importantly, *what states do depends upon what their identities and interests are, and identities and interests change.*

The myth 'anarchy is what states make of it' is associated with a branch of the constructivist tradition of IR theory. Constructivism argues that identities and interests in international politics are not stable – they have no pre-given nature. This is as true for the identity of the sovereign nation-state as it is for the identity of international anarchy. The important thing is to look at how identities and interests are constructed – how they are made or produced in and through specific international interactions (Onuf, 1989; Wendt, 1994).

Constructivism is among the most influential IR traditions of the late 1990s and early 2000s (Walt, 1998). This is in part because what it says seems to be just common sense. We know from our own individual experiences that today we are not *exactly* who we were yesterday, and we are unlikely to be *exactly* the same tomorrow. Our identities – who we are – change, as do our interests – what is important to us. Constructivism is so influential also because its myth 'anarchy is what states make of it' seems to 'build a bridge' between neorealist 'truths' and neoliberal/neoidealist 'truths'. There is something for everyone in constructivism. It provides the answers to all our IR problems.

But the success of constructivism depends upon an important move. The myth 'anarchy is what states make of it' means that states decide what anarchy will be like – conflictual or cooperative. By making the state the key decision-maker about the 'nature' of international anarchy, constructivism contradicts its own argument that identities and interests are always in flux. It allows that the *interests* of states – conflictual or cooperative – change. But by making the character of international anarchy dependent upon what states decide to make it, constructivism produces the *identity* of the state as decision-maker, *and this identity cannot be changed*. If the identity of the state as decision-maker were questioned, the constructivist myth 'anarchy is what states make of it' would not function.

The myth 'anarchy is what states make of it' was proposed by one of the leading constructivist IR theorists of the 1990s and early 2000s, Alexander Wendt, in his 1992 essay 'Anarchy is What States make of It: The Social Construction of Power Politics'. In this chapter, I will summarize the argument Wendt makes in support of his myth and focus explicitly on how he stabilizes the decision-making character of the state to functionally guarantee the 'truth' of his myth. I will turn to the film *Wag the Dog* as my interpretive guide for a functional critique of Wendt's myth.

Wag the Dog is a comic film about producing a phony war to distract the US public's attention from the troubles of its president. As such, the film illustrates how the producing function of identities and interests works. Production works by not letting people see the moves behind the scenes that make what is produced – whether that is a phony war or an IR myth – appear to be true. Production, in other words, works though seduction – through 'withholding something from the visible' (Baudrillard, 1987:21), even though there may be nothing to see.

The neorealist anarchy myth is a seductive myth. With its emphasis on the *structure* of international anarchy, it seems to withhold from view the *authors* of this structure of international anarchy. Seduced by neorealism, Wendt asks the obvious question, 'who is the author of international anarchy?' And he gives us his answer – socially constructed states. But, as the film *Wag the Dog* implies, maybe asking 'who is the author?' is the wrong question. Maybe a more interesting question is 'how do practices work to make us believe there is an author of international anarchy?'

What does the myth say?

In his 1992 essay 'Anarchy is What States make of It' (reprinted 1995), Alexander Wendt takes as his point of departure the classic dispute between realists and idealists – updated as neorealists and neoliberals – over the behaviour of states in international politics. Must state behaviour be conflictual, as neorealists argue, or might it become increasingly cooperative, as neoliberals hope? A lot of how you think about state behaviour, Wendt tells us, depends upon how you think about the 'nature of international anarchy'. Is it a structure that puts constraints on state behaviour so that competition and conflict are guaranteed and much cooperation is ruled out (Waltz, 1979; see Chapter 2 above)? Or is it a place in which processes of learning take place among states in their everyday interactions so that more cooperative institutions and behaviours result (Kegley, 1993; see Chapter 3 above)? Wendt claims that the debate about international anarchy boils down to a debate about which of these two aspects of anarchy theorists decide to stress – structure or process.

Yet however much neorealist and neoliberal scholars divide on the issue of structure vs. process, they share three things in common. Wendt claims that all of these theorists agree that (1) states are the dominant actors in international politics; (2) rationalism is the theoretical disposition through which they explain international state interactions; and (3) security is defined in 'self-interested' terms (Wendt, 1995:130; see Table 4.1). While Wendt doesn't seem to find any problems with the state-centricism of these traditions, he does have worries about their rationalism and the very different ways they think about self-interest.

Wendt worries that the neorealist and neoliberal commitment to rationalism restricts how theorists can think about international change. He suggests that 'rationalism offers a fundamentally behavioral conception of both process and institutions: they change behavior but not identities and interests' (Wendt, 1995:129–30). The problem with rationalism, then, is that it takes the identities and interests of

Table 4.1 What do neorealists and neoliberals agree and disagree about?

Agree	Disagree
1 States are the dominant actors in international politics	Whether to emphasize structure (as neorealists like Waltz do) or process (as neoliberals like Kegley do) when explaining state interactions in international anarchy
2 Rationalism is the theoretical disposition through which international state interactions are explained	
3 Security is defined in 'self-interested' terms	

states as given, thereby welcoming questions about changes in state behaviour but *not* being open to questions about changes in state identities and interests.

This is a problem for Wendt because it restricts how IR theorists are able to think about the notion of 'self-interest'. Neorealists think of self-interest in terms of 'self-help'. As we saw in the Waltzian myth 'international anarchy is the permissive cause of war', self-help defines the behaviour of states in a system of structural anarchy – one in which there is no orderer. Self-help flows from the structural arrangement of international politics. According to Waltz, it is not an institution that can be changed. Therefore, states cannot learn to overcome the limits of international anarchy – the deterministic structure of anarchy that makes states look out for themselves in order to survive. All they can learn to do is to adjust to these limits of anarchy. As Wendt puts it, in this system 'only simple learning or behavioral adaptation is possible; the complex learning involved in redefinitions of identity and interest is not' (Wendt, 1995:130). This limit to state learning is imposed by thinking about international anarchy in neorealist terms *which are also rationalist terms*.

Wendt suggests that these limits on thinking about changes in state learning are found in 'weak' liberal arguments as well because such liberals 'concede to neorealists the causal powers of anarchical structure', even while they argue that processes of learning can take place within neorealist-defined anarchy. But other liberals – those he terms 'strong liberals' – want to move away from simple learning to complex learning, from thinking only about changes in state *behaviour* to theorizing changes in state *identities and interests*. Wendt's sympathies lie with these 'strong liberals'. Yet he laments that because of their commitment to rationalism, 'neoliberals lack a systematic theory of how such changes occur and thus must privilege realist insights about structure while advancing their own insights about process' (Wendt, 1995:131; see Box 4.1). If only there were a theory that would allow them to take structure seriously by recognizing that 'transformations of identity and interest through process are transformations of structure' (Wendt, 1995:131). And, guess what, there is such a theory – Wendtian constructivism (Wendt, 1995:131–2).

Constructivism might not only offer neoliberals the theory of change they need to be able to privilege process over structure, but because it takes structure seriously it might also be able to 'build a bridge' between neorealism and neoliberalism (Wendt, 1995:132; Wendt, 1994). And if that can be done, then maybe we won't have to choose

> **Box 4.1 What's wrong with rationalism, according to Wendt**
>
> 1 Rationalism takes the identities and interests of states as given because it recognizes changes in states' behaviour but not changes in states themselves (i.e. their identities and interests)
> 2 Rationalism also takes the identities of and the interests generated from international anarchy as given. For rationalists, neither the structure of international anarchy nor the self-help system it is said to produce can be changed
> 3 Overall, rationalism limits theoretical understandings of change in agents and structures because it only examines changes in behaviour and excludes an examination of changes in identities and interests

between defining the character of international anarchy as either predominately conflictual or predominately cooperative any longer. But to get to this place, we have to recognize that the character of international anarchy is not pre-given but the outcome of state interactions and that self-help is not an immutable feature of international anarchy. Wendt puts it like this: 'There is no "logic" of anarchy apart from the practices that create and instantiate one structure of identities and interests rather than another; structure has no existence or causal powers apart from process. Self-help and power politics are institutions, not essential features of anarchy. *Anarchy is what states make of it*' (Wendt, 1995:132; italics in the original).

How does Wendt make his argument that there is no logic of anarchy and that self-help is an institution that can be changed rather than one that determines the behaviour of states? He does so by challenging the neorealist logic of anarchy, a logic which makes self-help an unalterable aspect of international anarchy, one that leads to competition and conflict. And he does this by reclaiming a place for *practice* in international politics (see Figure 4.1).

Wendt argues that, whatever one may think of Waltz's overall argument in *Man, the State and War* (1954), this early attempt by Waltz to understand international anarchy left a place for state practice that was written out of his *Theory of International*

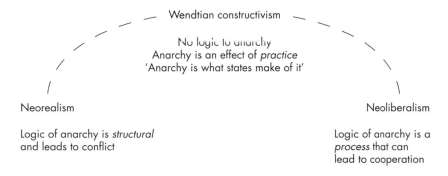

Figure 4.1 Wendt's constructivist bridge between neorealists and neoliberals

Politics (1979). In Waltz's early book, international anarchy is what allowed wars to occur, but something else always had to happen – some first- or second-image practice by states. But in the later book, international anarchy became a structural principle that made states behave competitively and often conflictually, making first- and second-image explanations of war seem unnecessary (Wendt, 1995:133–4; see Chapter 2 above). According to Wendt, the place of practice can and must be reclaimed within this 'neorealist description of the contemporary state system as a competitive, self-help world' (Wendt, 1995:134). And, if practice is recovered, we can accept this description of the world *without* accepting its explanation of competitive and conflictual state behaviour as a necessary structural outcome. Put differently, by restoring an emphasis on *practice* among states, Wendt believes he will be able to recover *process* among states – processes that may transform international anarchy from necessarily either conflictual (for neorealists) or cooperative (for neoliberals) into 'what states make of it' (Wendt, 1995:134).

How Wendt recovers practice and process within this neorealist description of international politics is by arguing that there are at least two structures that explain state behaviour in international politics. The first, which has been Wendt's focus so far, is international anarchy. The second is 'the intersubjectively constituted structure of identities and interests in the system' (Wendt, 1995:138). If we acknowledge only the first structure of international anarchy, we pretty much end up with Waltz's neorealist explanation of international politics or, alternatively, a 'weak liberal' argument that, even within structural anarchy, some cooperative behaviour is possible. If, however, we include the second intersubjectively constituted structure of identities and interests, then international anarchy is not necessarily either conflictual or cooperative.

So, how does Wendt think about this intersubjectively constituted structure of identities and interests? Wendt takes states as his point of departure. States are the fundamental actors in international politics. These state actors 'acquire identities – relatively stable, role-specific understandings and expectations about self' (Wendt, 1995:135) through their relationships with other actors and the meaning structures they find themselves in. 'Identities are the basis of interests' which are once again constructed relationally (Wendt, 1995:136). Moving from actors to identities to interests, we finally end up with institutions. 'An institution is a relatively stable set or "structure" of identities and interests' (Wendt, 1995:136). 'Institutions are fundamentally cognitive entities that do not exist apart from actors' ideas about how the world works' (Wendt, 1995:136).

Wendt is not trying to make a 'which came first' argument – identities or institutions. He is trying to say that identities, interests, and institutions all result from interactive, social processes and that they are 'mutually constitutive' (Wendt, 1995:137). We may think institutions are 'already there' because we rely upon them to orient our behaviour, but institutions are not pre-given. They are constituted through social interactions among identities. Similarly, identities are not pre-given either, but are formed through interactions with other identities and with collective social institutions.

What does this mean for Wendt's myth 'anarchy is what states make of it'? It means that even if we accept the neorealist description of the world as an anarchical, self-help world, by supplementing this anarchical structure with the intersubjectively constituted structure of identities and interests, then neither anarchy nor self-help are meaningful terms prior to the social interactions of states. Anarchy and self-help only become meaningful once social interactions have taken place. And, because 'people act toward objects, including other actors, on the basis of the meanings that the objects have for them' (Wendt, 1995:135), and because the objects of 'anarchy' and 'self-help' have no meaning prior to state interactions, we will only know if anarchy and self-help will lead to conflict or cooperation once we know what states do socially (Box 4.2).

Taking these two structures together, what can we say about state behaviour in a competitive, self-help anarchical system prior to social interaction? We *cannot* say it will be necessarily conflictual or cooperative. We *can* say, according to Wendt, that states will try to survive (Wendt, 1995:139). But how they will achieve that survival is an open question.

With all this in mind, Wendt invites us to think of an example in which two actors who have no prior social contact stumble upon one another and want to ensure their continued survival. His example is the arrival of aliens on earth. Wendt asks, 'Would we assume, *a priori*, that we were about to be attacked if we are ever contacted by members of an alien civilization? I think not' (Wendt, 1995:141–2). Yes, we'd be cautious, he argues, but we would probably not want to appear to be threatening to the aliens unless they were first threatening to us, as we would want 'to avoid making an immediate enemy out of what may be a dangerous adversary' (Wendt, 1995:142). We would read the alien's social signals before deciding whether we would behave conflictually or cooperatively. And, importantly, Wendt argues 'we would not *begin* our relationship with the aliens in a security dilemma; security dilemmas are not given by anarchy or nature' (Wendt, 1995:144).

The same is true of sovereign states in their social interactions. On first meeting, two states (which Wendt refers to as 'alter' and 'ego') have no reason to assume the worst of one another. Yes, they each want to survive and to preserve their own unique ways of being states – of organizing their systems of governance. But none of this suggests that they are in a 'security dilemma' in which self-help principles prevail. States do not *necessarily* have to increase their power to increase their security because every other state poses a threat to them. 'Social threats are constructed, not natural' (Wendt, 1995:141). Prior to social interaction, there is no such thing as a

---

Box 4.2 Three fundamental principles of constructivist social theory

1 'People act toward objects, including other actors, on the basis of the meanings that the objects have for them': SOCIAL KNOWLEDGE
2 'The meanings in terms of which action is organized arise out of interaction': SOCIAL PRACTICE
3 'Identities [and interests] are produced in and through "situated activity"': SOCIAL IDENTITIES AND INTERESTS

Source: Wendt, 1995

social threat. It is identities that produce collective meanings like social threats, and 'identities are produced in and through "situated activity"' (Wendt, 1995:144).

If, in this particular situated activity, the only prior interest states have is to survive, then this means that it is not *a priori* in a state's interest to make a social threat. A state (alter) may choose to make a social threat, or ego may interpret alter's actions as threatening. But prior to social interaction, alter and ego are not in a security dilemma. Wanting to survive in no way guarantees that alter or ego will behave conflictually towards one another. Nor, of course, does their interest in survival guarantee they will cooperate. Anarchy is what alter and ego make of it (see Table 4.2).

Additionally, Wendt adds, 'If states find themselves in a self-help system, this is because their practices made it that way. Changing the practices will change the intersubjective knowledge that constitutes the system' (Wendt, 1995:144). So even if alter and ego make anarchy conflictual by creating a self-help system, they can always escape this self-help system by changing the ways they think about and then act in this system. This is why Wendt argues 'that the meaning in terms of which action is organized arise out of interactions' (Wendt, 1995:140). And Wendt

Table 4.2 Three stories of international anarchy

	Realism	*Idealism*	*Constructivism*
Actors	States	States	States
Goals	Survival	Survival	Survival
Actors' behaviour in anarchy	Increase power to ensure survival	Promote social learning through: • institutions (e.g. UN) • ideas (e.g. democracy and liberal capitalism)	Unpredictable prior to social interaction
What mitigates state behaviour?	Self-help because • no world government (anarchy) • cooperation among states unreliable	International society	Intersubjectively constituted structure of identities and interests • if state identities and interests produced as competitive → competition • if state identities and interests produced as cooperative → cooperation
Logic of anarchy	Conflictual	Cooperative	Anarchy is what states make of it

goes on to make this point explicitly, by illustrating how 'identities and interests are transformed under anarchy: by the institution of sovereignty, by an evolution of cooperation, and by intentional efforts to transform egoistic identities into collective identities' (Wendt, 1995:133).

But probably the most important move Wendt makes in his essay is not found in his critique of rationalism or in his critique of self-help. Rather, it is in his *lack* of a critique of state-centrism. He acknowledges that making the state the focus of his analysis may strike some theorists, especially postmodernists, as 'depressingly familiar' (Wendt, 1995:163). But, of course, it is only by keeping the state as the central decision-maker in his constructivist explanation of international politics that Wendt can conclude that 'anarchy is what states make of it'.

Wendt defends his state-centricism on the grounds that 'the authorship of the human world' must not be forgotten. For to forget the author is to risk reifying the world – to make it an object that is already there that actors relate to rather than to recognize it as a 'world of our making' (as another constructivist with a different take on constructivism, Nicholas Onuf, puts it; Onuf, 1989; Wendt, 1995:147). Wendt is critical of realists for reifying the structure of international anarchy. He puts it like this: 'By denying or bracketing states' collective authorship of their identities and interests . . . the realist–rationalist alliance denies or brackets the fact that competitive power politics help create the very "problem of order" they are supposed to solve – that realism is a self-fulfilling prophecy' (Wendt, 1995:148). But anarchy is not a problem external to states. It is produced through the 'competitive identities and interests' states create through their everyday activities. 'It is what states have made of themselves' (Wendt, 1995:148). This is a strong argument for accepting the authorship of the state – for viewing anarchy as a product of state activities rather than as a self-help, competitive structure that traps states into behaving conflictually towards one another.

The film *Wag the Dog* illustrates the moves in Wendt's constructivist myth. It demonstrates how identities, interests, and institutions are intersubjectively constituted. And it seems to support Wendt's point that reifying or forgetting the authorship of acts can have dangerous consequences – even leading to war (or the perception of war at least). Either way, real people die. Authorship, it seems to suggest, must be transparent for democratic institutions to operate properly. It must withhold nothing from view. It must not be seductive.

But *Wag the Dog* also makes us wonder if production/authorship can ever be effectively separated from seduction – if authorship can ever be transparent. If not, then we have to ask what the seduction of authorship does. Wendt's answer, as we know, is authorship reifies what authors supposedly make (like anarchy). *Wag the Dog*'s answer is more complicated. It's answer is this: yes, seduction reifies production – not just of what authors supposedly make but of authors themselves. And, this answer goes on, this reification of authorship is terribly clever because there is no guarantee practices can reliably be traced to authors.

Wag the Dog

Wag the Dog opens with a joke that appears on the screen.

'Why does a dog wag its tail?'
'Because a dog is smarter than its tail. If the tail were smarter, the tail would wag the
    dog.'

The film then cuts to a less-than-slick television commercial, in which a couple of
jockies discuss why they will support the president in the up-coming election – they
know it is unwise to 'change horses in midstream'. Cut to exterior of the White House.
Cut to interior of the White House. A man in a rumpled hat, raincoat, and suit has
arrived. He looks ordinary enough (apart from the fact that he is Robert De Niro).
He makes his way into the bowels of the White House, into a safe room in which he
is the focus of a crisis meeting. He is Conrad Brean or 'Mr. Fix It', as the president's
assistant Winifred refers to him. Conrad/Connie is briefed on the current crisis.
A Firefly Girl has alleged sexual misconduct against the president while she was
alone with the president in the oval office.

    The president's campaign opponent, Senator Neal, already has word of the
story and is ready to run a new campaign commercial. Connie and his team view
the new spot in the crisis room. The spot pans a crowd of what we suppose are the
president's supporters cheering. A subtitle asks a question that is also spoken in
a voice-over, 'In the final days of the campaign, has the president changed his
tune?' The commercial cuts to the exterior of the White House as we hear Maurice
Chevalier singing 'Thank Heaven for Little Girls'. The commercial cuts back and
forth between this exterior shot and an interior shot of the president's empty desk
chair in the oval office. The voice-over continues, 'The Presidency is about honor, it's
about principles, and it's about integrity. This tune has got to change. On election day,
vote Neal for president.'

    Mr. Fix It goes to work. The election is 11 days away. All he has to do is distract
the public's attention from this sexual crisis long enough to ensure the president is
reelected. How he decides to do this is by changing the story – by inventing
something the US public will find more gripping than this sexual scandal. He decides
to delay the president's return from China and start a series of rumours about non-
existent weaponry and a non-existent war to distract the public. He explains his plan
to the president's staff in a pretend dialogue between a staff member and a newspaper
reporter.

Connie: Whoever's leaking that stuff to that geek at the *Post* lets it slip.
      Gees, I hope this won't screw-up the B3 programme.
      What B3 programme and why should it screw it up?
      Well, if the president decides to deploy the B3 before it's fully tested. . . .
      Deploy the B3 before it's fully tested? Why?
      Why? The crisis?
Winifred [interrupting Connie's imaginary dialogue]: What crisis?
Connie: Well, I'm workin' on that. [Carrying on with his plan, Connie continues.]

At the same time, get General Scott of the Joint Chiefs of Staff and pour him on a plane right away to Seattle. He's all flustered and nervous to talk to the Boeing people.

Winifred: Right [to Connie]. Do it [to an assistant].

Assistant: But, but. . . .

Connie: But what?

Assistant: But there isn't a B3 bomber.

Connie: Where did you go to school kid, Wellesley?

Assistant: Dartmouth.

Connie: Then show a little spunk. There is no B3 bomber. General Scott to the best of your knowledge is not in Seattle to talk to Boeing.

Winifred: It won't work, Connie. It won't prove out.

Connie: It doesn't have to prove out. We've just gotta distract 'em, just gotta distract 'em. We've got less than two weeks until the election.

Winifred: What in the world would do that? What in the world would do that?

Connie: I'm workin' on it. I'm working on it.

What Connie comes up with is a way to 'change the story, change the lead' by creating the 'appearance of a war' between the US and Albania – a country that (at the time this film was made, prior to the war in Kosovo) the US public knows very little about. He and Winifred fly to Hollywood to enlist the aid of film producer Stanley Motss because, as Conrad puts it, 'War is showbusiness'. When it becomes clear to Stanley that Connie wants him to help with the 'war', Connie tries to explain to him what kind of help he has in mind.

Stanley: And you want me to do what?

Connie: We want you to produce.

Stanley [expressing shock and disbelief]:   You want me to produce your war?

Connie: It's not a war. It's a pageant. We need a theme, a song, some visuals. We need, you know, it's a pageant. It's like the Oscars. That's why we came to you.

Stanley: I never won an Oscar.

Connie: And that's a damn shame you didn't, but you produced the Oscars.

Stanley [getting the idea]:   It's a pageant.

Connie: It's 'Miss America'. You're Bert Parks.

Connie's pitch for a US war with Albania convinces Stanley who sets about producing it – its script revolves around Albanian terrorists trying to smuggle a nuclear bomb into the US via Canada in a suitcase; 'news footage' of an 'Albanian girl' escaping from rebels in Albania which is leaked to the press and run on all the news programmes; choreographing the president's return from China at which time he is given an offering of thanks by a small 'Albanian girl and her grandmother'; not to mention a couple of songs and countless merchandizing tie-ins. And all of it is consumed by television viewers as real.

And then, the 'war' 'ends'.

Senator Neal, the president's electoral opponent, announces on television that he has evidence from the CIA that the war is over. Stanley is upset.

Plate 4.1 Presidential aide Winifred and 'Mr. Fix-It' (Connie) visit Hollywood producer Stanley Motss in his Los Angeles home. Winifred feeds dialogue supplied by Stanley to a White House press spokesperson he is watching on television as evidence of her and Connie's production of news and events.
© New Line Cinema Productions, Inc.
Source: http://www.wag-the-dog.com/photos

Stanley [angry]: He can't end the war. He's not producing this.
Connie [exasperated]: The war's over guys.
Stanley: No!
Connie [now matter-of-factly]: It's over. I saw it on television.
Stanley: No, the war isn't over 'til I say its over. This is my picture. This is not the CIA's picture. . . .

But then Stanley devises a scheme to keep productive control of 'his picture' even though someone else ended 'his' war. He tells Connie, 'This is nothing. This is nothing. This is just "Act I: The War". Now we really do need an "Act II".' He continues

Plate 4.2 Stanley learns that Connie wants him to 'produce the war' between the US and Albania.
© New Line Cinema Productions, Inc.
Source: http://www.wag-the-dog.com/photos

to spin the war story, now taking place after the war has officially ended. He decides there is a US soldier trapped behind enemy lines who doesn't know the war is over. He has been separated from his unit. US forces will now mobilize to rescue him. Proud of himself, Stanley tells Connie, 'Bottom of the 9th [swings an imaginary baseball bat]. Alright? Alright? They don't know who they're playing with. They don't shut down our picture.'

And so the show goes on, even when the US soldier they 'cast' as the hero turns out to be a psychotic imprisoned for raping a nun, even when the 'hero's' return is delayed because the plane he, Connie, Stanley, and Winifred are travelling in crashes, and even when the 'hero' is killed by a shopkeeper because he is trying to rape the shopkeeper's daughter. Stanley simply scripts a patriotic funeral for the returned 'hero'. And the story holds long enough to ensure the president's reelection.

What does all of this tell us about the world of *Wag the Dog*? How does this film make sense of the world? What does it say is typical and deviant in that world?

The world of *Wag the Dog* is a made-in-the-media world. TV shows and news broadcasters define reality, even to the extent that they make us believe that the US is at war with Albania. And because television is where reality happens, television is the only place reality can be transformed. For example, early in the film the CIA confront Connie and Winifred with 'the facts' that there is no evidence of a war in Albania or of any Albanian nuclear device in Canada. But this is not enough to 'end

Plate 4.3 In an office above the sound stage where the 'patriotic funeral' of a 'US soldier' who 'fought' in the Albania conflict is being broadcast to a grateful US public, Connie and Stanley congratulate one another on a job well done.
© New Line Cinema Productions, Inc.
Source: http://www.wag-the-dog.com/photos

the war'. The only way the war can be ended is the way it was started – on television. Connie articulates this when he declares the war is over because 'I saw it on television'.

It is through the medium of television that information and ideas are disseminated. And, more importantly, what this practice of dissemination does is construct and reconstruct identities, interests and institutions in the world of *Wag the Dog*. Stanley is reconstructed from a Hollywood producer into a producer of a war with an interest in keeping 'his' picture going until he can bring it to some poignant closure. The US public are constructed as patriots with an interest in beating the Albanians and securing the US borders. The institution of war is transformed from something that occurs in places like Albania, the US, and Canada into something that occurs in televisual spaces. All of these identities, interests, and institutions co-construct one another. It all seems to illustrate the 'intersubjectively constituted structure of identities and interests' (Wendt, 1995:136) of which Wendt writes (Box 4.3).

And as the mediatic magic of war replaces both the upcoming presidential election and the president's alleged indiscretion with a Firefly Girl as the only tale in town, the film seems to invite us to take the notion of tales – and tails – as seriously as it does. What's all this preoccupation with tales, tails, and wagging about anyway?

One way to approach this question is by asking another – what is typical and what is deviant in the world of *Wag the Dog*? And seeking an answer to this question takes us back to the joke that the film opened with – 'Why does a dog wag its tail? Because a dog is smarter than its tail. If the tail were smarter, the tail would wag the dog.' In light of this joke, the film's title, and the film's plot, it seems fair to conclude that what is typical in the world of *Wag the Dog* is for the tail to wag the dog, and what is deviant is for a dog to wag its tail.

All of this encourages us to ask 'who is the dog and who is the tail?' It is this sort of question that Wendtian constructivism gives into. One answer might be that the dog is the US public and the tail is the politicos of Washington who employed Connie, Stanley, and Winifred. Another might be that the media wag the politics who wag the public. Either way, the US public is constructed as being wagged all the time – as that which is constructed. In contrast, the tail decides how the wagging will be performed. The tail (politics/media) is the author of the tale (story) about the war (see Table 4.3).

One might think of *Wag the Dog* as a clever parable of Wendt's myth 'anarchy is what states make of it', rewritten as something like 'war is what producers make of it'. Either way it is phrased, the moral is the same. And this moral is the very one Wendt evoked in his defence of a state-centric/actor-centric approach to understanding international politics. That defence was this – if we forget who the

---

Box 4.3 How does *Wag the Dog* make sense of the world?

Reality is produced, circulated, and transformed through the media, especially television. It is through the media that identities, interests, and institutions appear to be constructed and reconstructed.

Table 4.3 What seems to be typical and deviant in the world of *Wag the Dog*?

Typical	Deviant
For the tail (spin doctors and policy-makers) to wag the dog (the US public)	For the dog (the US public) to wag its tail (spin doctors and policy-makers)

author of practices is, then we cannot hold that author accountable. We end up responding to identities, interests, and institutions as if they were authored by no one. In *Wag the Dog*, we respond to staged events like war as if they were real, which gives them some reality. And, in international politics, we respond to 'the logic of anarchy' and its accompanying self-help security dilemma as if they were real, thereby giving them some reality.

But identities, interests, and institutions are authored by someone, Wendt suggests. Authorship is always at the bottom of production. It is only by keeping the author in mind that we can hold the author accountable and, maybe even more importantly, recognize that we are the authors of our own lives. Anarchy is what states make of it. War is what producers make of it. Our lives are what we make of them.

Wendt's warnings about the dangers of reification are echoed in the film by Stanley, the Hollywood producer. Stanley asks Connie, 'Where do movies come from if nobody produces them, Connie? Where do they come from?' Stanley asks this question because his tale about war, a hero's triumphant return, and the hero's patriotic funeral seem to come from nowhere. But Stanley knows they result from production, and he is the producer. Throughout the film, Stanley waxes philosophically about production. Producing is problem-solving:

Stanley: If you've got a problem, solve it. That's producing.

Producing is heroic:

Stanley: Producing is being a samurai warrior. They pay you day in, day out for years so that one day when called upon you can respond, your training at its peak, and save the day.

And producing is invisible:

Stanley: Thinking ahead. Thinking ahead. That's what producing is.
Connie: It's like being a plumber.
Stanley: Yes, like being a plumber. You do your job right, nobody should notice. But when you fuck up, everything gets full of shit.

But it is this last aspect of production – its invisibility – that makes it so problematic both for Stanley and for Wendt. According to Stanley, production only truly functions when it is seductive – when it withholds its own acts of production from view. For production to work, nobody should notice. While Stanley knows this about production and producers, it is also what bothers him about production. He has never won an Oscar because, as he tells Connie, 'There is no Oscar for producing.' Producing is never recognized. It is always invisible. So when his 'patriotic pageant' is winding up, he quarrels with Connie because he finally wants proper recognition for the work he has done.

Connie: You can't do it.
Stanley [angrily]:   Don't you tell me that. Don't you ever tell me that. I'm the producer

of this show. [Looks out the window at the set where the patriotic funeral of the returned war hero is being shot.] Look at that. That is a complete fucking fraud, and it looks 100% real. [contemplatively, softly] It's the best work I've ever done in my whole life, because it's so honest . . . [insistently] I tell you, for once in my life I will not be pissed on. I want . . . I want the credit. I want the credit.

Stanley knows that if he is allowed to have 'the credit', the whole picture will fall apart. He just doesn't want to accept what he knows about production when it comes to credit. He knows production is only revealed when there's a problem. When there is no problem, production and the producer are out of sight. And because they are out of sight, we long for them. We want to see the processes of production and the producer who is pulling all the strings. But, as *Wag the Dog* makes explicit, the deal is we can have our entertaining movie only if we suspend our interest in the processes of production and in the producer.

In this sense, production is always tied to seduction. That's the deal. The story/film/tale teases us into wanting what we cannot see – what is seductively withheld from the visible – while at the same time it promises not to show us too much. For if we knew about all the special effects and all the dramas behind the drama, we would lose interest in the drama itself. That's why it is so hard to be a producer – because the deal is that you can never take the credit. If you do, the audience will be disillusioned with your production, so any 'credit' for that job well done will dissolve.

What Stanley knows about production is the same thing Wendt knows. Just as the invisibility of Stanley's role as producer guarantees that his tale about war appears to be true, the invisibility of the state's role as producer guarantees that neorealism's tale about international anarchy appears to be true. By 'exposing' states as the producers/decision-makers who make international anarchy, Wendt ensures that the neorealist anarchy tale ceases to function as if no one authored it.

Stanley and Wendt both implicitly understand that production is tied to seduction. But neither of them seems to know that seduction doesn't necessarily conceal an author. *Seduction doesn't just tease us into wanting what we cannot see. It convinces us that there is something there to see.* It fools us not only about what might be a 'real' or a 'false' tale. *The tale itself tricks us into thinking that there is an author of the tale.*

For Wendt, as for the film *Wag the Dog*, asking 'who is the author?' is an important question to guard against the evils of reification. And for Wendt at least, it is a necessary question. For it is by asking the question of authorship that Wendt gets us out of the neorealist anarchy myth by emphasizing state *practices* in the production of international anarchy. But I wonder if this is where the constructivist emphasis on practice should be placed. Because the film raises another question: Does the tail wag the dog or does the *tale* wag the tail that *appears* to wag the dog? Put differently, is anarchy what states make of it or do *practices* (which Wendt does not consider) make states that *appear* to make anarchy?

Practice, seduction, and dead authorship

Wendt's myth 'anarchy is what states make of it' gets us out of the neorealist anarchy myth in which international anarchy determines that states will compete to ensure their survival, relying upon self-help logics. Wendt gets us here by emphasizing practice in international politics – specifically, how the practices of socially constructed states make international anarchy into what it is, whatever that may be. So Wendt emphasizes practice by emphasizing what states *do*. In this sense, Wendt's socially constructed states are the tails that wag international anarchy. They are the authors of anarchy. But there are other practices that Wendt ignores, and these are the practices that construct states themselves as decision-makers which then go on to make international anarchy. This second set of practices concern tales/stories rather than tails/actors. On this reading, tales or stories construct states as tails/authors who then wag/make anarchy.

It is only by excluding this second set of practices – the practices that construct states as decision-makers or producers of international anarchy – that Wendt can claim states as the authors of anarchy. Put differently, the tale/story must go without saying for Wendt's own constructivist tale 'anarchy is what states make of it' to function.

But in the mediatic world of *Wag the Dog* and in the Wendtian world of constructivism, the tale/story is a bunch of practices that no one ultimately controls.

Think about it. Ask yourself the question 'who is the ultimate decision-maker in the film?' Several answers present themselves.

The answer is not Stanley. If for no other reason, we know this because when Stanley refuses to let the picture roll without credits – when he makes it clear he cannot abide by the agreement that he can never tell anyone about what he has done – Connie authorizes the government thugs to kill him.

So does that make Connie the author/decision-maker? He certainly seems to be the 'real' producer. He is the one who came up with the story. He is the one who initially organized it. He just delegated some of this authority to Stanley. So maybe Mr. Fix It is the real centre of decision-making power in the film.

Except this answer doesn't hold up because we know that just as Connie delegated decision-making responsibility to Stanley, the president delegated decision-making authority to Connie. So is the president ultimate decision-maker in the world of *Wag the Dog*? Some might answer yes. I would answer no.

My answer is there is not necessarily a decision-maker behind the scenes. And this answer comes from thinking once again about how the film makes sense of the world. As I mentioned before, the film makes sense of the world through the media. It is the circulation of ideas/stories/tales through the media that constructs reality and tells us what to think. And, throughout the film, the president, Connie, and Stanley are always responding to the mediatic presentation of events, trying to come up with problem-solving solutions to them. But trying to solve a problem – what Stanley calls producing – is only a response. It means that production is driven by *practices* – by the mediatic representation of the tale. The tail/producer, then, doesn't wag the dog/public. The tale/practices wags the tail/producer so that it appears that the tail/producer wags the dog/public (Table 4.4).

Table 4.4 Reconsidering what is typical and deviant in the world of *Wag the Dog*

Typical	Deviant
For the tale (mediatic practices) to wag the tail (producers/spin doctors/policy-makers) so that it *appears* that the tail (producers) wags the dog (US public)	Either: • for the dog (US public) to wag its tail (producers/spin doctors/policy-makers) Or: • for the tail (producers/spin doctors/policy-makers) to 'really' wag the dog (US public) without being wagged by the tale (mediatic practices) itself

Consider these examples. The president needs to bring in Connie to fend off a political crisis before the election because the news media will run the story of his alleged sexual misconduct with the Firefly Girl the next morning. The tale/story drives the president's decision to employ Connie. Connie understands that tales – not tails – wag dogs. And so he invents another tale to rival the tale of the president's alleged sexual misconduct. His tale is a US war with Albania. Senator Neal, appreciating how tales are wagging tales now, intervenes to put a stop to his electoral opponent's strategy. He doesn't do this by saying 'there is no war', even though he clearly has the 'evidence on the ground' that there is no war because he has been consulting with the CIA. No, he recognizes that it would be political suicide to speak the 'truth' that there is only a mediatic war. So he spins another tale to the tale to the tale – that the war is about to end. By ending the war on television, Senator Neal ends the war. Never mind that Stanley insists this is his war and no one else can end it. The war is over because what happens on television is real.

Examples like these abound in the film. Indeed, the whole film is framed from beginning to end through the media. The film opens with a campaign commercial supporting the president and it ends with the following television special report, 'A group calling itself Albania Unite has claimed responsibility for this morning's bombing of the village of Close, Albania. The president could not be reached for comment, but General William Scott of the Joint Chiefs of Staff said he has no doubt we'll be sending planes and troops back in to finish the job.' What do these two media bookends tell us about the mediatic world of *Wag the Dog*?

Obviously, beginning and ending a film with television spots testifies to the importance of mediatic practices in the world of *Wag the Dog*. But it does more than this. There is a movement depicted in the film from thinking you can reliably trace the authorship of mediatic events back to an author to knowing you cannot. The opening campaign spot seems easy enough to trace. It is an advertisement for the president paid for by the campaign to reelect the president. But what about the final special news bulletin. Who authored that? It wasn't Stanley because Stanley is dead. It is unlikely to be either Connie or the president because Connie's job was over when the president's reelection was assured, and that occurred before this special report. So who is the author? Is it the media itself? Maybe in part but never entirely, because as the world of *Wag the Dog* showed us, the media are always responding to stories/tales.

So, as the film ends, we are left with the tale still spinning and no one on to whom we can pin the tale/tail, so to speak. Authorship is unreliable. We'll keep searching for authors because the seductive practices of production make us believe we might find them one day. But no amount of wanting authors to be findable or authorship to be more reliable will make it that way. Authorship cannot be guaranteed. In the end, we only have a tale – a bunch of practices that gave us not only the illusion of a war but the illusion of an author/producer/decision-maker behind the war.

What does this all mean for Wendt's constructivist myth 'anarchy is what states make of it'? It means that however well intentioned Wendt is in trying to give us an escape from some reified 'logic of anarchy', he only succeeds at getting us out of a deterministic conflict/cooperation debate by determining the character of the state. In other words, *Wendt only manages to escape the reification of international anarchy by reifying the state as decision-maker.*

Wendt can allow that states can change roles – from producers of conflict to producers of cooperation, for example, just as Stanley changed roles from producer of films to producer of a war. But Wendt cannot tell us how states get produced as producers. *His constructivism draws the line of taking practice seriously under the state.* States can make practices, but – however much he might claim the contrary – Wendt's constructivism *does not allow* states to be produced. They are already there. They have to be. They are the producers of anarchy. 'Anarchy is what *states* make of it.'

Wendt's constructivist myth 'anarchy is what states make of it' is a comforting myth. It promises to free us from deterministic logics of anarchy. It claims to build a bridge between neorealists and neoliberals. And, most importantly, it answers the seductive question 'who is the author of international anarchy?' and gives us an author – states. IR theorists want all of this. And that is why Wendtian constructivism has been so popular among IR theorists.

But by accepting these benefits of Wendtian constructivism, we are also accepting its liabilities. And constructivism has at least two major liabilities. First, it fails to deliver on its promise to take us beyond reification because, in order to escape a reified logic of anarchy, it reifies the state. Second, by reifying the state – by insisting on the state as the author/decision-maker of all tales – constructivism misses the opportunity to deliver on another of its promises, to restore a focus on process and practice in international politics (see Table 4.5 on p. 79). *Wag the Dog* suggests to us that it is a more interesting question to ask 'how does an actor *appear* to be a decision-maker/producer/author?' than it is to ask the seductive question 'who is the real decision-maker/producer/author?'

This constructivist compromise does allow us to hold states accountable for any wagging of international anarchy they may be doing, and that is an important contribution to the anarchy debates. But it prevents us from investigating practices that produce states as producers. With Wendtian constructivism, we think we understand how states as tails function in international politics. But, as *Wag the Dog* reminds us, wagging isn't mostly about tails/states. It's about tales/practices.

Table 4.5 Advantages and disadvantages of the Wendtian compromise

Advantages	Disadvantages
Can hold states accountable for their part in producing anarchy as either conflictual or cooperative	• Cannot escape reification because Wendt replaces a reified logic of anarchy with reified states • Misses the opportunity to restore a broad focus on process and practice in international politics because Wendt must exclude from consideration the practices that make states as products of anarchy in order for his myth to function

Suggestions for further thinking

Topic 1 Constructivism

Nicholas Onuf was the first to introduce the concept of constructivism into the IR theory debates. Onuf made his case for constructivism in his 1989 book *World of our Making*. Since then, several theorists have adopted and adapted constructivism, in ways unanticipated by Onuf (as he suggests in his 1999 essay). Wendtian constructivism is the best known. Recently, Wendt consolidated and clarified his position in his book *Social Theory of International Politics*. Others, like John Ruggie, have applied constructivism to readings of international politics. And the Onuf school of constructivism has carried on apace. It is not surprising, then, to read in the pages of *Foreign Policy* that constructivism is a necessary tool in any IR theorist's toolbox, an argument made by Stephen Walt.

Suggested reading

Nicholas Greenwood Onuf (1989) *World of our Making*. Columbia: University of South Carolina Press.

—— (1999) 'Worlds of our Making: The Strange Career of Constructivism in IR', in Donald J. Puchala (ed.) *Visions of IR*. Columbia: University of South Carolina Press.

Alexander Wendt (1999) *Social Theory of International Politics*. Cambridge: Cambridge University Press.

John G. Ruggie (1998) *Constructing the World Polity*. London: Routledge.

V. Kublakova, Nicholas Greenwood Onuf, and Paul Kowert (eds) (1998) *International Relations in a Constructed World*. New York: M.E. Sharpe.

Stephen M. Walt (1998) 'International Relations: One World, Many Theories', *Foreign Policy* (Spring): 29–46.

Topic 2 Postmodernism

One of the things that makes constructivism so appealing to many IR theorists is that it is *not* postmodernism. Yet it was postmodernist arguments, introduced to IR theory in Richard Ashley's pathbreaking critique of neorealism and through a series of essays by R.B.J. Walker (many of which are collected in his book *Inside/Outside*), that got IR scholars thinking about questions of identity and practice to begin with. While constructivist scholars turned to scholars like Anthony Giddens for their insights about international politics, poststructuralist scholars turned to the works of Michel Foucault, Jacques Derrida, Jean Baudrillard, and Julia Kristeva, among others.

There are long-running debates between constructivists and poststructuralists (both termed 'reflectivists' by Robert Keohane) about identity, practice, and politics. While Wendt's constructivist myth 'anarchy is what states make of it' arguably de-naturalizes the logic of anarchy with its focus on state practice and thereby enables us to hold states accountable for behaviours which produce either conflict or cooperation, poststructuralists criticize this sort of constructivism because it cannot interrogate the practices that produce states themselves. Some IR scholars have criticized poststructuralism for being apolitical because it does not identify actors and hold them accountable in traditional ways (as Wendtian constructivism does). Yet poststructuralists argue that it is precisely their insistence *not* to ever stop investigating how power is used to stabilize identities that makes their work political (see George and Edkins) and makes some constructivist work (like Wendt's) politically vacuous in contrast.

As this discussion should make clear, it is a poststructualist position that informs my critique of Wendt's anarchy myth in this chapter. To use this chapter to highlight the differences between constructivist and poststructuralist approaches to states as the authors of international anarchy, a useful poststructuralist work to assign is Michel Foucault's essay 'What is an author?'

Suggested reading

Richard K. Ashley (1984) 'The Poverty of Neorealism', *International Organization* 38 (2):225–86.

R.B.J. Walker (1993) *Inside/Outside: International Relations as Political Theory*. Cambridge: Cambridge University Press.

Robert O. Keohane (1988) 'International Institutions: Two Approaches', *International Studies Quarterly* 32:379–96.

Jim George (1994) *Discourses of Global Politics: A Critical (Re)introduction to International Relations*. Boulder, Col.: Lynne Rienner.

Jenny Edkins (1999) *Poststructuralism and International Relations: Bringing the Political Back In*. Boulder, Col.: Lynne Rienner.

Michel Foucault (1984) 'What is an Author?', in Paul Rabinow (ed.) *The Foucault Reader*. New York: Pantheon, pp. 101–20.

Gender

Is gender a variable?

What's an IR scholar to do about feminism? This is a question that has troubled IR scholars for decades. While feminist debates engaged people in social and political spaces outside the discipline of IR, IR scholars did their best not to see the relevance of feminism for their own debates. That didn't stop some feminists from rethinking key IR concepts like power through feminism (Carroll, 1972), but such contributions were largely ignored by IR scholars until recently (Murphy, 1996; Pettman, 1998). It was only in the late 1980s, when feminist questions pushed their way on to the IR agenda through books, journals, and conferences, that feminism suddenly seemed attractive to IR scholars.

And then, for a few years, IR's affair with feminism flourished. Feminist essays were added to IR journals, feminist panels were added to IR conferences, and feminist jobs were added to IR departments. In the early 1990s, feminist questions – questions about the presumed gender neutrality of international politics from the standpoint of women – seemed to have been added to most aspects of IR.

But its affair with feminism did not always go smoothly. Even though IR scholars (mostly men) began to welcome feminist contributions (mostly from women) into their field and even though some men even proclaimed themselves to be feminists, (mostly female) feminists were not always happy with the terms of this relationship. They kept pointing out to IR scholars (men and women) that feminist questions could not just be added to and stirred in with IR questions in ways that left the core of the discipline unchanged. They stressed that feminist questions changed the very terms in which IR was approached, understood, and studied. Furthermore, they pointed out that feminist questions were every bit as legitimate and important as IR's classical approaches to war and peace.

Needless to say, not everyone welcomed these feminist insights. While the era of dismissing feminists and feminist questions from IR debates without political risk had now passed, surely feminists must realize that the point of feminist approaches to IR was to further IR's core agenda of asking questions about war and peace and not to de-stabilize the very foundation from which such questions were asked. Sometimes feminists just went too far, it seemed to (mostly male) IR scholars, to the point that feminists seemed to be out of control altogether because they insisted on asking the wrong and the most uncomfortable sorts of questions. Certainly, (mostly male) IR scholars could still advise (mostly female) feminists on how to do feminism in a way that was compatible with IR and comfortable for IR scholars. And so they did (Keohane, 1989; Weber, 1994).

One effect of IR's paternalistic engagements with feminists and feminist questions was to decrease the scope of feminist questions that IR scholars had to take seriously (Zalewski, 1993 and 1995). Feminist questions, it seemed, should not be asked about everything all the time. There seemed to be a place and a time when feminist questions mattered and when feminists should be heard. Feminism deserved a 'proper' place in IR debates, but it was (mostly male) IR scholars who placed feminism – who put and kept feminism in its place (Zalewski, 1999). But feminism rarely stayed in its place. And that troubled and sometimes even scared IR scholars. How could feminism more reliably be placed as a complement to IR questions?

In 1996, a solution for placing feminism presented itself in the form of Adam Jones's essay 'Does "Gender" make the World Go Round? Feminist Critiques of International Relations'. Uniquely for a male IR scholar, Jones seems to argue that the problem with feminism isn't that it is everywhere and has to be kept in its place. Rather, the problem with feminism is that it has limited its own contribution to the IR debates – the gender variable. By 'the gender variable', Jones does not mean some quantitative cause/effect quotient. Rather, the gender variable simply expresses what feminists study – or, as Jones argues, what feminists *ought* to study, which is gender.

Jones's use of the gender variable simultaneously expands and contracts feminist IR debates. On the one hand, it seems to open up IR by moving away from what Jones claims are narrow feminist questions about women and the feminine to broader gender questions about all genders. On the other hand, it makes feminism and feminists manageable because it places them within one reasonable realm – gender – and places gender itself within the confines of a variable. Now IR scholars can look at gender as a discrete set of relationships that they can explore qualitatively or quantitatively. And they can do so without forever having to answer feminist charges that they are just adding in gender to IR analyses. After all, it was feminists, Jones tells us, who gave us the gender variable. IR scholars are only putting it to proper use.

Like our (neo)idealist myth 'there is an international society' (Chapter 3), Jones's myth 'gender is a variable' is never defended by Jones. What is defended is the need to make feminist engagements with IR more balanced. And to do this, Jones argues, the gender variable must be made more inclusive, especially of the gendered positions of men and masculinities in international relations. In other words, if feminists want 'women's issues' and 'feminine concerns' to be considered in IR, then (mostly male) IR scholars are right to insist that 'men's issues' and 'masculine concerns' be given equal time. Yet in making this argument, the gender variable 'itself' simply goes without saying. It is simply the basis upon which Jones makes his argument for its expansion.

But is gender a variable? Gender *appears to be* a variable in Jones's essay because its status as a variable is never questioned. But what would it mean for gender to be a variable? It would mean that gender can be placed and contained in some distinct thing called a variable. And, because gender could be so placed, the gender variable itself would be outside of gender (Box 5.1).

All this makes Jones's myth 'gender is a variable' attractive to IR scholars because it seems to allow them to stand outside of gender while they analyse gender and the gendered relationships of international politics. Yet many feminists have resisted conceptualizations of gender as a variable precisely because they argue one is never outside of gender. Jones's myth 'gender is a variable' only functions so long as it can claim not just a gender-neutral status (equality to all genders) but a gender-free status (being outside of gender altogether). And here Jones runs into a problem,

---

Box 5.1 What would it mean for gender to be a variable?

1 Gender could be placed and contained in some distinct thing called a variable
2 This 'gender variable' would itself be outside of gender. It would be free of gender

because the effect of his use of the gender variable is to construct a gendered relationship between IR and feminism, a relationship in which feminism is once again placed in the stereotypical feminized position as irrational, unbalanced, and in need of male guidance. Left unchecked and unplaced, feminism threatens to destroy IR's family romance about man, the state, and war.

In this chapter, I will explore how Jones mythologizes the existence of gender as a variable by arguing that 'the gender variable' should be more balanced. I will focus on how Jones characterizes feminism, assesses feminism's contribution to the IR/gender debates, and argues for a more comprehensive notion of a gender variable which includes a focus on men and masculinities. Finally, I will reassess Jones's myth 'gender is a variable' through the film *Fatal Attraction*.

Fatal Attraction, the 1987 classic horror thriller about a heterosexual affair gone wrong, in many ways parallels IR's relationship with feminism. IR scholars are attracted to feminism just as Dan Gallager/Michael Douglas is attracted to Alex Forest/Glenn Close. But this attraction can be fatal to the classic family romance – in Dan Gallager's case about the heterosexual family; in IR's case about war and peace. It is only by placing the feminine Alex – by keeping her in her place – that Dan survives his fatal attraction to her. And it is only by presenting himself as outside of gender that Dan's placement of Alex seems to be acceptable, so much so that audiences cheer at her demise. But what if neither Dan nor IR can stand outside of gender? Then the myth 'gender is a variable' could no longer function because gender could not be isolated from how one sees the world, especially the world of gender.

What does the myth say?

Jones's essay begins with a common IR theme – that the classical tradition of international relations (realist–idealist debates that focus on questions of war and peace; see Chapters 2, 3, and 4 above) is experiencing challenges from a number of alternative approaches to IR, including feminism (1996:405). Jones's project is to assess whether or not the feminist challenge to the classical tradition has made a contribution to our knowledge of IR. His conclusion is mixed. On the one hand, he credits feminism for its 'seminal "discovery" of . . . the gender variable in international relations' (1996:407). On the other hand, however, Jones argues that 'feminism's standard equation of *gender*, an inclusive designation, with *women/femininity*, a narrower and more restrictive one', unduly limits what the gender variable is and should be in IR (1996:407). The gender variable, Jones argues, needs to be expanded to include other aspects of gender, notably men and masculinity (1996:420–9). Jones devotes his essay to making his case for the need to expand the gender variable.

But if Jones is to convincingly argue that the gender variable needs to be expanded, he must demonstrate that feminism's application of it is too restrictive. In making this case, Jones offers answers to three key questions: (1) What is feminism? (2) How have feminists made use of the gender variable in IR? (3) How should feminists and other IR scholars apply the gender variable in future?

What is feminism for Jones? Jones suggests that 'few schools of criticism are as diverse and diffuse as feminism' (1996:405). Even so, he identifies 'three essential features of feminist theories', while allowing that some post-positivist feminists might

Table 5.1 What is feminism for Jones?

Subject of feminism	Women as historical and political actors
Epistemology of feminism	Grounded in the realm of women's experiences
Normative agenda of feminism	1 Seek global transformations towards greater equality of women and the feminine because both are historically underprivileged, under-represented, and under-recognized 2 Equality for women and the feminine must overcome suppression of women by men as 'an international ruling class'

not accept all of these features (1996:406; see Table 5.1). In terms of their subject of analysis, all feminist theories 'focus on women as historical and political actors' (1996:406). In terms of how they conduct their analyses, all feminists share 'an epistemological foundation in the realm of women's experience' (original italicized; 1996:406). Finally, in terms of their normative outlook, all feminists contend that 'women and the feminine constitute historically underprivileged, under-represented, and under-recognized social groups and "standpoints"; and this should change in the direction of greater equality' (original italicized; 1996:406).

Later in his essay, Jones adds a forth point to his list of feminist features. He writes, 'It is fair to say that a very common motif, one that almost deserves inclusion on a list of feminism's defining features, is of *men as an international ruling class*, their internal squabbles secondary to the basic challenge of suppressing women' (1996:408).

What is wrong with feminism is also what, for Jones, is wrong with feminism's application of the gender variable in IR. Feminism's concern with women and the feminine make it too narrow, and its research programme is normatively based. It not only attempts to better women's lives, it seems to place the blame for the difficulties women face squarely on men (if Jones's fourth point is taken into account). And all of this adds up to suspect scholarship because it means that feminism is driven by a normative agenda. And this has no place in proper scholarship, according to Jones. Allowing a quote from Sara Ruddick to speak for all feminists, Jones argues that 'feminists are partisans for women' (Ruddick, 1989:235). But Jones reminds us that 'partisanship and scholarship do not always mix easily' (Jones, 1996:407).

To make his point that the partnership of feminist IR scholarship makes its use of the gender variable unbalanced – because it includes positive analyses of women and femininity but primarily negative, if any, analyses of men and masculinity – Jones offers a few examples of what he sees as feminist IR scholars' use of the gender variable. These serve as his answer to question 2 above, 'How have feminists made use of the gender variable in IR?' Jones's answer is, restrictively (Table 5.2).

Jones's conclusion that 'feminist attempts to come to grips with the gender variable remain limited, even radically constrained' (1996:406) follows from his illustrations of how what he has characterized as feminism has engaged with realism, the privileged pillar of the classical tradition. Jones identifies four themes/topics

Table 5.2 How have feminists made use of the gender variable?

Topic/Theme	Feminist argument	Contribution to IR?
Opposed dualisms	Male and masculine structures privilege men and exclude women. These structures must be supplemented 'by incorporating the gender variable', thereby creating more opportunities for women	No, because it blames men and masculinities for how the world is
Realist state	1 The state as either masculinist or male (radical feminist argument)	No, because it is an extreme and essentialist view of the state
	2 'The personal is political' (liberal feminist argument)	Yes, and it should be added to the three other levels of analysis – individual, state, and international
Rational-actor model	Labels of Western-style rationality as a peculiarly male/masculinist phenomenon reflecting and perpetuating patriarchal power. Can be corrected with sterotypical 'Mother Earth' essentialist ways of thinking about actors	No, because what the argument boils down to is that men and masculinity are essentially bad and women and femininity are essentially good
Realist conceptions of power and security	1 Expand the range of power relationships that realism considers	Yes, because gendered power relationships should be included in realism
	2 Redefine power	No, because it sneaks in feminist normative agenda by adding prescriptions about what power should be rather than descriptions of what power is

on which feminists have critiqued realism: (1) opposed dualisms; (2) the realist assumption of the state; (3) the rational-actor model; and (4) realist conceptions of power and security. Jones suggests that feminists are not alone in criticizing realism on these topics. But 'what is distinctive about the feminist orientation is the incorporation of the gender variable, and the exploration of its influence on women and (to a lesser extent) society as a whole' (1996:409).

So on the topic of opposed dualisms, when feminists critique realism for being 'inextricably bound up with a hierarchical world order', what feminists focus on is 'the extent to which Realist discourse perpetuates gender hierarchies along with hierarchies of class and state' (1996:410). Notwithstanding post-positivist feminist critiques that examine realism's construction of and construction through hierarchies, Jones places his emphasis here on liberal feminist engagements with realism because, as he argues, 'there are signs that it [liberal feminism] may be staging a comeback as some of the more paradoxical and stifling aspects of post-positivism become evident' (1996:410).

What do liberal feminists say about realism and gender hierarchies? According to Jones, these feminists argue that 'what is male/masculine is standard, universal, the measure by which everything *other* is judged' (1996:410). This has the effect of privileging men and masculinities in politics, economics, and academics. And so liberal feminism 'concentrates its efforts on *supplementing* classical frameworks by incorporating the gender variable' (1996:410). In practice, this means opening up structures that have 'ordinarily been a male preserve' to women (1996:410).

Turning to feminist analyses of the realist state, Jones (using the work of radical feminist Catherine MacKinnon) argues that feminists describe the state as either masculinist or male, which implies that the state cannot provide security for all of its citizens (Jones, 1996:412; MacKinnon, 1989:163). Jones dismisses feminists like MacKinnon for overstating their case (an argument, it should be added, made by many feminists as well). In contrast to radical feminism, Jones finds the liberal feminist argument that 'the personal is political' so persuasive that he recommends that it should 'supplement the triumvirate of "levels" guiding classical analyses of international affairs [individual, state, international, or as Waltz puts it, man, the state, and war; see Chapter 2 above]' (1996:413).

Concerning the rational-actor model that realism relies upon, Jones argues that again 'the distinctive feminist contribution here is the labeling of Western-style rationality as a peculiarly male/masculinist phenomenon reflecting and perpetuating patriarchal power' (1996:413). All he sees feminists offering to counter it are stereo-typical 'Mother Earth' essentialist ways of thinking about actors. And so, Jones concludes that feminists claim all women are good and all men are bad.

Finally, concerning realist conceptions of power and security, Jones claims that feminist contributions here take two forms. 'They may seek to illuminate the power relationships that standard commentary has overlooked; or they may propose a radical redefinition of what actually constitutes "power"' (1996:414). Jones approves of the former feminist way of engaging realist conceptions of power and security because, as Jones argues, they rightly draw attention to how the realist model that focuses exclusively on states or state elites 'misses a wide range of power relationships that discriminate against women' (1996:414). But he objects to feminist attempts to redefine power because he sees these as 'more prescriptive than descriptive' (1996:415), thus sneaking in feminism's normative agenda once more.

When these feminist critiques of realism are applied to questions of war and peace, Jones tells us, 'the plight of embodied women is front and centre throughout, while the attention paid to the male/masculine realm amounts to little more than lip-service' (1996:412). What all of this tells us is that feminists' use of the gender variable has been biased from the start against men and masculinities. This is not surprising considering that feminism, as Jones characterizes it, is a tradition that makes a gender-biased argument for a more femininely and womenly engendered world from the beginning. Feminism is unbalanced, even irrational, because of its normative, prescriptive agenda.

So, if this is the problem, how can it be corrected? How should feminists and other IR scholars apply the gender variable in future? Jones answer is to offer 'more balanced and fertile theories of the gender variable's operation in international relations' (1996:423) by supplementing the partiality of feminist gender analysis with an analysis of gender focused on men and masculinities. He puts it like this, 'My suggestions are feminist-grounded in that they seek to apply a core feminist methodology – isolation of the gender dimension of an issue or phenomenon. But they move beyond presently existing feminist approaches by directing the analytical beam equally toward the gender that is, so far by definition, under-represented in feminist commentary' (1996:424). Jones argues that his focus on men and masculinities is 'a necessary first step towards synthesis: a blending of gendered perspectives that will allow the gender variable and its operations to be examined in more multi-dimensional terms' (1996:424).

Jones offers a list of 'issue-areas and phenomena that could help generate real-world research agendas' for his more multi-dimensionally conceived notion of gender in IR. These include mostly 'public' topics – like how men are displaced as refugees during war, how men are murdered and commit suicide more than women, and how state violence including torture and incarceration overwhelmingly affect men rather than women. They also include a couple of 'private' topics like men taking risky and/or bad-paying jobs to support their families and being the victims of ethnic attacks (1996:424–9; see Table 5.3).

Overall, Jones's point is that men suffer disproportionately to women in international relations, and feminism occludes the gendered suffering of men because of its biased research focus on women and the feminine. Feminism's contribution of the gender variable is a good one, but it has been badly applied to investigations of IR because feminist prescriptions about how the world *should be* for women detract attention from how the world *is* for men.

The merits of Jones's argument – not to mention the (in)accuracy with which he characterizes feminism – are hotly debated, a point I will come back to later (see Carver, Cochran, and Squires, 1998; Jones, 1998; Zalewski, 1999). Yet however right or wrong Jones's argument about feminism's uses of the gender variable may be, all Jones's points assume the myth 'gender is a variable'.

Writing of the gender variable, Jones suggests that gender can be 'isolated' (1996:410, 424), 'incorporated' (1996:420), 'blended' (1996:424), 'balanced' (1996:

Table 5.3 How should feminists and non-feminists use the gender variable in the future?

Public issues and phenomena concerning men to be included	*Private issues and phenomena concerning men to be included*
1 Men as displaced war refugees	1 Men taking badly paid and/or dangerous jobs to provide for familes
2 Men as victims of murder and as suicides	2 Men becoming political victims because of ethnic conflicts
3 Men as victims of state violence, including torture and incarceration	

423), and 'broadened' (1996:406, 407, 429). In other words, gender is a discrete phenomenon that can be placed in IR. And it is those aspects of feminist IR scholarship that Jones can 'add' to IR – like the feminist emphasis on personal politics or feminist attempts to expand the range of power relationships that realism should consider – that he credits as genuine contributions to the world of understanding gender relations in international relations. These have a place in IR scholarship, unlike feminist attempts to disturb structures of realism and rationality or to redefine power, according to Jones (see Table 5.2).

And because some feminist insights can be added to/placed within IR scholarship, then 'the gender variable' can also be added. It can be expanded to include aspects of gendered international politics that Jones claims feminists ritually neglect. All of this is consistent with Jones's myth that 'gender is a variable'. That feminism has unduly restricted the place of gender in IR does not detract from Jones's myth that 'gender is a variable'. All it means is that the gender variable's placement and place must be reconsidered in view of gender studies of men and masculinities.

But what if 'placing' gender is not so easy as Jones suggests? *What if gender is not something to be placed or added to but something through which the world is viewed?* If gender is a way of seeing the world – a worldview – then it cannot be a variable, because a variable is something that is placed in a world. And it is as a worldview that feminist and gender scholars regularly describe gender. For example, consider the definition of one feminist, V. Spike Peterson, that Jones includes in his essay. Even though Jones quotes Peterson as evidence of his myth 'gender is a variable', Peterson instead writes of gender as a worldview.

> Feminist scholarship, both deconstructive and reconstructive, takes seriously the following two insights: first, that gender is socially constructed, producing subjective identities *through which we see and know the world*, and, second, that *the world is pervasively shaped by gendered meanings*. That is, we do not experience or 'know' the world as abstract 'humans' but as embodied, gendered beings. As long as that is the case, accurate understanding of agents – as knowable and as knowers – requires attention to the effects of our 'gendered states'.
>
> (Peterson, quoted in Jones, 1996:406; my italics)

Peterson's discussion of feminist scholarship and its conceptualization of gender have nothing in common with Jones's list of 'essential feminist features' (see Table 5.4). Furthermore, she discusses gender not as something that can be placed but instead as something that helps us to place things – events, people, ideas – that we encounter in our everyday world. If gender is a worldview, a perspective on the world, then no amount of arguing for the expansion of gender as a variable will make gender something that can be placed or, for that matter, kept in its place.

So why do IR scholars like Jones try so hard to 'place' gender? Could it be that they fear that their own privileged perspectives on international politics and their own centralized questions might be displaced – if not replaced – by feminist ones? Put differently, if left unchecked, might disruptive and inappropriate feminist questions disturb IR's traditional worldview, in which we see primarily 'man, the state, and war'?

Table 5.4 Jones's characterization of feminism vs. Peterson's characterization of feminism

Jones	Peterson
Feminism = normative programme	Feminism = worldview
Characteristics of Feminism: 1 Feminist subjects are women and the feminine 2 Feminist epistemology grounded in women's experiences 3 Feminist normative agenda is to promote women's equality and to blame men and masculinity for global injustices	Characteristics of Feminism: 1 Gender is socially constructed, producing subjective identities through which we see and know the world 2 The world is pervasively shaped by gendered meanings; therefore, we 'know' the world as gendered beings

The urgency to place gender – especially the feminine – and the question of whether gender can be placed are explored in *Fatal Attraction*. The film works hard to distinguish between good expressions of the feminine (mother/wife) and bad expressions of the feminine (vengeful lover) in order to leave undisturbed a worldview that makes us sympathetic to the plight of the male lead, a character who fears unbounded femininity. Yet to achieve these things, isn't the film told from a gendered point of view? And if this is the case, then the film raises the more general question, isn't any 'placing' of gender always a gendered placing? Put differently, isn't it impossible to stand outside of gender, especially when trying to put gender in its place?

Fatal Attraction

Fatal Attraction is a horror thriller in which what is at stake is the survival of the Gallager family, composed of Dan, his wife Beth, and their daughter Ellen. The horror genre of the film is established from the very first frame. The credits and title appear on a black background. No music plays. The background becomes the New York sky, and soon we see a very industrial skyline, unlike the typical New York cityscape filmgoers would recognize. Subdued city sounds are heard. As the camera takes us across the skyline to focus on the window of one apartment, the eerie city sounds are replaced by family sounds. We hear a children's television programme in which a woman and a small girl are conversing. Cut to interior of the apartment.

Beth Gallager, in T-shirt and underwear, is rushing about the room picking things up and encouraging Dan to hurry. Beth and Dan are going out to a party connected to Dan's work. Dan, also dressed in a shirt and underwear, is stretched out on a couch, listening to music through headphones while working on some papers. On an adjacent couch, daughter Ellen in pyjamas and robe watches the television. The family dog rests its sleeping head on Ellen's lap. The wife of another couple who wants to know what Beth will wear to the party rings. They coordinate outfits. Ellen plays with her mother's makeup, and Beth cleans her up. Dan asks where his suit is, Beth tells him, and there he finds it freshly dry-cleaned.

The contrast between what is outside the Gallager's apartment and what is inside could not be more stark. Outside is danger, represented by scary sounds and eerie landscapes. Inside is the comfort and routine which comes with a traditional family arrangement. Everything outside is unsettling. Everything inside is safe and secure, made possible by Dan's work outside the home and Beth's work as a homemaker.

But insecurity is quickly introduced into the Gallager family through Alex Forest, a single woman who Dan briefly meets at the party that evening and who, we learn later, lives in the eerie warehouse part of the city. We first see Alex when Dan's friend Jimmy makes a pass at her. Alex gives him the coldest of looks. Jimmy says to Dan (who sees all this), 'If looks could kill . . . [giggling]', foreshadowing the danger Alex embodies. Later, Dan and Alex meet by chance at the bar. They are surprised, a bit embarrassed, and they laugh nervously as they recognize one another.

Dan [laughing]:   No, I'm not sayin' anything. I'm not even gonna look.
Alex [also laughing]:   Was it that bad?
Dan [still laughing]:   Well, let's just say I was glad I wasn't on the receiving end of that one.
Alex [lightly]:   I hate it when guys think they can come on like that.
Dan: Ah, Jimmy's OK. He's just a little insecure like the rest of us.

Dan begins this last comment looking straight ahead, but when he gets to the part about insecurity, he turns and looks right at Alex. The move is charming, even seductive, as revelations of male insecurity often are. Alex clearly finds Dan to be charming. Dan introduces himself, and Alex and Dan begin a conversation. Then Beth beckons Dan from the corner of the room.

Dan: I have to go.
Alex: Is that your wife?
Dan: Yup.
Alex [coyly, making a joke of it]:   Better run along [giggles].

Dan and Beth leave. When they get home, Beth, undressing in the bedroom, says to Dan, 'Aren't you forgetting something?' Dan, like us, seems to take Beth's words as a sexual advance. Beth then points to the dog who needs walking. When Dan returns, he finds his daughter Ellen in bed with Beth. Dan looks disappointed, and Beth, smiling, tells him, 'It's just for tonight, honey.' The price of domestic bliss is stereotypically spelled out for us, as it is for Dan, and that price is passion.

The next morning, Beth and Ellen go off to the country to look at a house Beth is interested in. She has long wanted to move the family to the country. She and Ellen will be away for the night. Dan stays behind because he has a rare Saturday meeting. As it happens, Alex is also at the meeting. She is the editor of a publishing company Dan's law firm is representing. After the meeting Alex and Dan again run into one another by chance. Caught in the rain and unable to get a taxi, Dan suggests they go get a drink together. They end up having dinner and discussing the possibility of taking the evening further.

Alex: Where's your wife?

Dan: Where's my wife? [surprised by the question]. My wife is in the country visiting her parents for the weekend.

Alex: And you're here with a strange girl being a naughty boy.

Dan: I don't think having dinner with somebody is a crime.

Alex: Not yet, anyway.

Dan: Will it be?

Alex: I don't know. What do you think?

Dan: I definitely think it's gonna be up to you [laughing nervously].

Alex: We were attracted to one another at the party, that was obvious. You're on your own for the night, that's also obvious. We're two adults. . . .

Dan [hardly able to get out the words]:   I'll get the check.

And so their passionate weekend begins. First we see the famous scene in which they have sex on top of Alex's kitchen sink full of dirty dishes (and we think, Beth only uses her sink to clean the dishes). They move into the bedroom, and when they finally speak, Alex says 'That was great.' And Dan keeps saying, more to himself than to her it seems, 'Thank God. Thank God.' They go out dancing, return to Alex's apartment, and have sex in the elevator. Dan spends the night. He returns home and learns that Beth won't be home that night as expected. And so, with Alex's persuasion, he spends the day with her, bringing the family dog with him. But as Dan prepares to leave after dinner and sex, Alex asks him to stay. When he won't, she slits her wrists and then tells him she is sorry if she has upset him. Dan stays to look after her.

From this point on, the cool, collected, careerist Alex becomes increasingly weird. She starts by harassing Dan with phonecalls and visits, behaviour which is not out of the question for someone who feels hurt and scorned and who wants to let Dan know their brief affair has left her pregnant. But then, when Dan rejects her, her behaviour turns dangerous. Alex pours acid on Dan's car, kidnaps his daughter for an afternoon, and, in a scene reminiscent of Hichcock, boils his daughter's bunny. In the film's climax, the over-the-top Alex attacks Beth in the bathroom of the family home, only to be nearly drowned by Dan and finally shot and killed by Beth. The film's closing shot is of the family photo of Dan, Beth, and Ellen. Family life for the Gallagers has finally been rescued.

Even though it is Alex who is killed in the film, it is Dan who is portrayed as the film's fearful victim. Indeed, *Fatal Attraction* – like any good horror film – is a paranoia picture, and the paranoia belongs to Dan. But, unlike classical horror films, Dan's paranoia is not introduced into the plot in reaction to something Alex has done. It is something Dan has felt since he was a small child. The film discloses this early on. As Dan and Alex share an evening together during their weekend-long affair, they listen to the opera *Madame Butterfly*. They both agree that this is their favorite opera. And then Dan reminisces, 'My father told me she was gonna kill herself. I was terrified.'

While Dan's confession foreshadows Alex's suicide attempt and her ultimately suicidal attack on Beth, which results in Alex's death, it does more than this. It begs the question, why was he terrified? Terror seems an unlikely response – even for a young boy – to the information his father has given him. Sad, sorry, upset, even relieved. But terrified? What did this boy have to fear? What does Dan have to fear now? And why – if the conclusion to this opera was so terrifying for young Dan – is it his favorite opera as an adult?

As the film jumps from romance to suspense to horror, it answers these questions. What Dan fears is what the film stereotypes as unbounded female emotion – an irrationality that turns Dan into a victim of Alex's vengeful anger when Dan tries to end their affair. But this unbounded female emotion also releases Dan's passion, something the film shows him experiencing only with Alex and never with his wife Beth (Conlon, 1996). This makes his attraction to Alex understandable. Yet because of his affair with Alex, Dan's family romance with Beth and Ellen is nearly shattered. For Dan, that is pretty scary. His attraction to Alex could be fatal to his sense of family.

All of this points to how the film makes sense of the world (Box 5.2). The world of *Fatal Attraction* is a world in which there is no higher value than living in a secure heterosexual nuclear family. This legitimate family gives meaning to one's life. This is the case as much for Alex as it is for Dan. For without a legitimate family (a marriage, a child), a woman like Alex is not valued. She is someone with whom a married man like Dan can have an affair and discard – or at least she *should* be and *would* be if she respected the implicit rules pertaining to affairs with married men. But Alex is not your typical woman. She is located outside of the reasonable limits of the heterosexual nuclear family – the only context in which reasonable behaviour is portrayed in the film.

Fatal Attraction works hard to present Alex as irrational. Never mind that Alex is a successful New York editor, a woman who controls her own life and her own body. None of this gives her life meaning because, the film tells us, legitimate meaning comes only from legitimate family. When Alex discovers she is pregnant with Dan's child, her hopes for a legitimate family seem to compel her down the path of increasingly bizarre behaviour. Remember the acid, boiled bunny, kidnapping, and attempted murder. Each irrational gesture has its basis in her lack of a legitimate place in a legitimate family. Woman on her own, the film tells us, is a mess.

This is in contrast to how the film portrays both Beth and Dan. If Alex is irrational because she is a woman out of place, Beth is a reasonable woman struggling to hold on to her legitimate place in the heterosexual family. She is a good wife and a good mother. She seems to have no responsibilities beyond those created by the marriage and the marital home. She makes Dan's life easy, and for this she is rewarded with legitimacy. By killing Alex, it is Beth who rescues her family (see Table 5.5).

Box 5.2 How does *Fatal Attraction* make sense of the world?

By valuing the traditional heterosexual nuclear family

There is no higher value than living in a secure family

This legitimate family gives meaning to one's life

Table 5.5 The place of woman in *Fatal Attraction*

	Legitimate woman (Beth Gallager)	Illegitimate woman (Alex Forest)
Place	Within the heterosexual nuclear family	Outside the heterosexual nuclear family
Characteristics	Good wife Good mother	Independent personally and professionally. This independence is coded in the film as barrenness and failure
Behaviour	Rational	Irrational

Dan, too, is a character in place. Forget his (irrational?) fear and attraction to a woman out of place. Dan is a rational man with a successful career as a lawyer and a traditional marriage. Even though he has an affair with Alex, he makes it clear from the beginning that this affair is not to interfere with his marriage. This is a reasonable position. And he falls back on 'adult agreements' and 'rules' whenever he finds it necessary to keep Alex in her place.

But so long as Alex seems to be safely in her place, Dan feels free to pursue his affair with her. We see this in a scene in which, shortly after their weekend together, Alex appears in Dan's office to thank him for 'not running away' when she slit her wrists and to invite him to the opera as a way of saying thank you. Dan refuses. Alex accepts this refusal, gets up to leave, and extends her hand for Dan to shake in farewell. But Dan embraces her instead while (in the director's cut of the film) Alex utters, wonderingly, 'When does no mean no?' It seems that 'no' only means 'no' when Dan fears he cannot keep Alex in her place.

That fear of not being able to keep Alex in her place begins during their lovers' weekend. Dan gushes on about his family life, explaining to Alex how lucky he is. Alex asks, 'So what are you doing here?' Dan's only reply is, 'Boy, you know how to ask the wrong thing.' This is illustrated in another scene, this time after Alex turns up at Dan's apartment, meets his wife, and secures his unlisted phone number and new address. Afterwards, Alex (who Dan now knows is pregnant with his child) tells Dan, 'I'm not gonna be ignored', and she asks Dan 'what are you so afraid of?' Dan gets increasingly agitated and casts Alex as hysterical.

Dan: You're so sad, you know that, Alex.
Alex: Don't you ever pity me, you bastard.
Dan: I'll pity you. I'll pity you because you're sick.
Alex: Why? Because I won't allow you to treat me like some slut you can bang a couple of times and throw in the garbage?

Dan says nothing in reply.

In contrasting Dan's and Alex's responses to their affair, the film tells us what is typical and deviant in the world of *Fatal Attraction* (Table 5.6). What is typical is for the heterosexual nuclear family to be respected as the only legitimate – and therefore reasonable – source of meaning. What is deviant is for this family

Table 5.6 What is typical and what is deviant in the world of *Fatal Attraction*?

Typical	Deviant
To respect the heterosexual nuclear family as the only legitimate and reasonable source of meaning	To disturb the heterosexual nuclear family though outside, irrational, and illegitimate influences

romance to be disturbed by outside, irrational, and illegitimate forces – like a pregnant, discarded mistress. This does not mean that a man like Dan cannot have the occasional affair. It does mean that whatever he does his behaviour must not pose a threat to his family life with Beth, Ellen, the dog, and that poor bunny. This point is emphasized in Dan's confessional scene to Beth. Beth does not get angry when she learns that Dan had an affair with a woman he does not love. But she is irate when she learns that Dan has impregnated Alex because Alex's illegitimate claim to a family with Dan now threatens Beth's legitimate family.

Dan's mistake is not that he had an affair. His mistake is that he had an affair with *Alex* – a woman who does not respect reasonable limits, a woman who does not stay in her place, a woman who does not behave as Dan assumed she would. And for this viewers generally feel sorry for him. Poor Dan. OK, he might not be the best guy in the world because he cheats on his wife. But this Alex woman is a maniac!

The film tells us that femininity must be kept in its place. One way of placing femininity is by securing it within a traditional domestic setting through a traditional marriage. This is where we find Beth. The only other rational ways to place it, the film tells us, are either to ignore it (which Dan fails to do) or to kill it. And of course, the demanding, irrational Alex as a woman out of place trying to weasel her way into the Gallagers' traditional family ends up dead. By concluding with the family photo, the film tells us that family life – what is traditional – can be rescued, so long as the feminine is kept in its place one way or another.

Fatal Attraction is a popular, anti-feminist response to feminism. Its message is that women like Alex – independent, demanding, and out of place – have gone too far. When woman and the feminine are out of place, all hell can break lose. And when it does, it is at the expense of things traditional (like the family) and of the traditional leaders of things traditional (men).

Fatal Attraction also tells us that if we now have to take gender issues seriously – like those that arise for a 'liberated' woman like Alex Forest – then we had better not forget that gender is a problem for men like Dan Gallager as well. Put differently, if Alex's 'personal is political', then so is Dan's. Dan has a family to support. That can be boring and passionless sometimes, and, because of this, Dan seeks sexual excitement with Alex. But he is first and foremost a family man who wants his family life to be respected, unthreatened, and unchanged.

Dan's mistake is that he thinks he can 'add' Alex/passion/unbounded feminine emotion to his life without changing it. Dan's mistake is the same mistake IR makes with feminism. It thinks it can 'add' feminist and gender issues to IR without upsetting the core issues of the discipline of IR and how they are studied. *Fatal Attraction* is very clear about why Dan thinks he can get away with keeping Alex in her place. It is because the film is told from Dan's point of view, made legitimate by the film's coding of the traditional heterosexual nuclear family as the only legitimate source of meaning. We are introduced to events through Dan's family. We follow Dan's life. We sympathize with Dan's character. *Fatal Attraction* is Dan's story. Feminists would argue that, told from Dan's point of view, *Fatal Attraction* is far from a gender-neutral tale. It is the tale of one man's reaction to unbounded feminine emotion (the film's symbolic equivalent for feminism) which he views as unbalanced and excessive. And his reaction is a reasonable one – and one with which we sympathize – because it is grounded in Dan's (and many viewers') respect for the traditional family. If you doubt this, recall that Alex has a very different story to tell about her affair with Dan, one that the film works hard to de-legitimize.

Because *Fatal Attraction* is only able to place Alex as the symbol of feminist excesses by telling its story from the point of view of Dan Gallager, the film raises the question, Does IR theory tell its story about feminism and the gender variable from a particular point of view? And, if so, What is Jones's point of view?

Placing feminism in IR?

Jones believes that 'the gender variable' needs to be more balanced because it occludes objective consideration of issues concerning men and masculinities in international politics. Jones credits feminism with introducing gender issues into IR. But he faults feminists for restrictively analysing gender in IR. Their normative focus on women and the feminine means that they either neglect or disparage men and the masculine. For Jones, feminism has a gendered perspective – women and the feminine. And that gendered perspective is what limits the contribution feminism could make to IR debates. By 'adding' men and masculinities to the gender variable, Jones claims to be correcting feminism's unbalanced perspective.

If Jones's myth 'gender is a variable' (not to mention his claim that feminists' use of the gender variable is unbalanced) is to function, it must be indebted to no particular gendered point of view. It must stand outside of gender and of any potentially gendered or genderable perspective. It must be neutral, a partisan for no one and nothing. It must be objective and non-normative. In other words, it must be all those things Jones accuses feminism of not being.

But just as *Fatal Attraction* tells its story about placing gender from a particular perspective, so too does Jones tell his. Of course, Jones tells the story of feminism and IR's implicit need to place it in a variable from his own perspective. But what makes Jones's perspective so compelling? What gives it meaning? What makes us think, 'yes, this guy has a point?' Just like Dan Gallager's story, Adam Jones's story is told in defence of a cherished tradition. For Dan, it is the traditional heterosexual nuclear family. For Jones, it is IR's classical tradition of realist/idealist treatments of questions of war and peace. *It is only because the classical tradition is the only place in which legitimate meaning is located that Jones's story about feminism's meaningless and unfair excesses makes sense.* And it is only because feminism is taken to be full of excesses that it must be placed in 'the gender variable' and replaced with what Jones sees as a more balanced gender variable – one balanced by attending to men and masculinities, by the way the world of IR really is rather than how feminists wish it to be (see Table 5.7).

Table 5.7 Gendered perspectives in *Fatal Attraction* and traditional IR theory

	'Fatal Attraction'	Traditional IR theory
Point of view	Dan Gallager's	Adam Jones's
Perspective	Traditional – legitimate meaning is based on the legitimacy of the heterosexual nuclear family	Traditional – legitimate meaning is based on the legitimacy of the classic IR tradition's treatment of questions of war and peace
How feminine/feminist 'excesses' are managed	• added through an illegitimate affair • ignored • killed	• added through the 'gender variable' • feminist work inconsistent with Jones's characterization of the 'gender variable' are ignored • feminine/feminist 'gender variable' replaced by (killed off with) a more 'balanced' gender variable that reemphasizes men and masculinities

Jones is relatively up front about his privileging of the classical tradition in IR as the standard against which any feminist 'contributions' will be judged. He opens his article by reminding us that 'In the last two decades, the classical tradition in international relations has come under sustained attack' and declaring that he wants to evaluate the merits of the feminist attack (1996:405). He couches the objective of his article in relation to the classical tradition: 'This article seeks to provide an overview of some major contributions and features of feminist IR thinking, with particular attention to the problem of war and peace that has attracted adherents of the classical approach more than any other' (1996:406). And then he evaluates feminism in terms of what it has 'added to' the classical approach (1996:408–20).

What is so interesting in Jones article, though, is that the article itself refuses to recognize that 'the classical approach' might not be a neutral point of view. It is like Dan's view of the traditional family and an affair in relation to it. *Any* reasonable person would see things exactly as Dan sees them, the film suggests. Similarly, Jones seems to suggest that any reasonable person would see the classical tradition's approach to questions of war and peace as just what IR is about. Consider our first three myths. All of them are firmly within the classical tradition, focusing as they do on questions of war and peace among sovereign nation-states in international anarchy. But none of these myths questions the classical tradition itself – the institutionalized context which makes questions of war and peace and mainstream approaches to investigating them meaningful.

Yet that is exactly what feminism does. It questions the classical tradition *itself*. Like Alex Forest, it is not content to simply accept the 'rules of the game' as already established by traditional social arrangements. Feminism, like Alex, asks of the classical tradition the 'wrong questions', like what makes these questions and approaches meaningful?; how are these meanings related to one another hierarchically?; and how do these meanings enable us to make value judgements that help us to place people and things as legitimate or illegitimate? (see Box 5.3).

These sorts of questions are dangerous to the classical approach to IR because they expose IR's classical tradition as not (necessarily) value-neutral or as a partisan for no one. And it is Jones who warns us that 'partisanship and scholarship do not always mix easily' (1996:407). Just as a feminist perspective has a normative agenda, feminists would argue, so does the classical approach. And that normative agenda, they would argue, is one that privileges subjects and sexualities that are constructed as 'normal' – heterosexual married men would be one example; masculinist understandings of reason, another. And feminists go further than this. They ask, is this the way things should be? Should normatively masculine ways of understanding the world and judging the value of things in the world continue to be the only legitimate ways of seeing the world? By posing these questions, feminists would argue, they are not ignoring men and masculinities but thinking about them critically. As such, they would argue, feminism provides a corrective to the tendency in IR to see *only* men and masculinities and see them in an unreflective light. Feminists have politically chosen to take a self-consciously 'biased' view of the world to compensate and hopefully transform traditional ways of seeing the world that occlude women and femininities as well as non-normative men and masculinities. At least they are open about their 'partisanship', they would argue, unlike proponents of the classical tradition.

By being unapologetic about its normative claims and by suggesting that all traditions have normative claims (disclosed or undisclosed), feminism jeopardizes everything near and dear to the hearts of proponents of the classical tradition. They can no longer ignore feminism, because that would be 'politically incorrect'. But they can still do their best not to take it seriously. How Dan refuses to take Alex seriously in the film is by caricaturing her as a stereotypical female hysteric. She is a nutcase. Unsurprisingly, Jones does the very same thing (if in milder terms) to IR feminists. He casts them as 'unbalanced', a nicer way of saying they are 'irrational' (1996:423). And, in the terms in which they must be understood from the perspective of the classical approach, they 'are'.

Box 5.3 The 'wrong' questions feminism asks of traditional IR theory

1 What makes traditional IR questions and approaches meaningful?
2 How are these meanings related to one another hierarchically?
3 How do these meaings enable us to make value judgements that help us to place people and things as legitimate or illegitimate?
4 What is traditional IR theory's normative agenda, and how does it use gender to secure this agenda while *appearing to be* gender-neutral and gender-free?
5 Should normatively masculine understandings of the world be the only legitimate ways of seeing the world?

But that is one of feminism's points. It is only because the classical tradition has a particular gendered point of view – one that necessarily sees most feminist questions as threatening and therefore stereotypes them as femininely unbalanced – that its proponents like Jones can 'place' feminism at all. Recall Peterson's description of feminism. For Peterson, feminism is a worldview that investigates how 'gender is socially constructed, producing subjective identities through which we see and know the world' and 'the world is pervasively shaped by gendered meaning' (1996:406). If one cannot know the world except from a gendered perspective, as feminists argue, then it is impossible for there to be either a gender-neutral or a gender-free standpoint from which to view the world. How Jones *sees* feminism – as unbalanced and in need of guidance from the classical tradition (guidance he provides) – betrays that Jones's way of seeing the world, *especially* the world of gender, is itself traditionally gendered.

If gender is not a place but a worldview, then it is not surprising that Dan Gallager cannot keep Alex Forest in her place outside the marital relationship any more than Adam Jones can keep feminism in its place inside a 'gender variable' in its relationship with IR theory. Alex will not stay in her place because her 'role' is a disruptive one in the Gallagers' traditional family romance. It isn't that Alex has anything against the traditional family. Clearly not, for she wants to have one herself with Dan. But once Dan crosses the line and invites her into his life, Dan cannot manage her as 'a discrete relationship' (Jones, 1996:423) that can be added to his life when he wants it and forgotten about when he doesn't. For better and for worse, Alex changes everything about Dan's familial relationships. Interestingly, it is not Dan but Beth (the good anti-feminist girl) who ultimately deals with Alex (the bad feminist girl) and re-secures the Gallagers' traditional family.

It's similar for feminism and IR. IR's attempts to place gender are doomed to fail because gender is not a discrete relationship that can be added to IR when (mostly male) IR scholars decide they can control it and ignored when they decide they can't. Feminist questions are scary for IR scholars in the classical tradition because they don't allow IR scholars to ignore their own normative – and gendered – perspectives. And for this Jones gives them 'the gender variable' as their '"seminal" discovery' (1996:423) – a place within IR from which they can reasonably get on with the work of doing gender. Jones's move is a sort of proposal to IR feminists. You can join the classical tradition on legitimate terms and enter the traditional family as full, legitimate members, he seems to tell them, so long as you give up on your de-stabilizing behaviour. Be Beth, a domesticated but happy anti-feminist. Don't be Alex, a 'free' but unhappy (and ultimately dead) feminist. What urkes feminists most about Jones's 'proposal' is that he claims it is 'feminist-grounded' (1996:424), when the only ground it protects is that of the classical tradition.

Even so, feminists point out that Jones's gendered moves to domesticate feminism in a variable all evidence what makes Jones's myth 'gender is a variable' function. Jones only recognizes the gendered claims of feminism, claims feminists never try to conceal. Jones, on the other hand, fails to recognize his own gendered claims, claims that give meaning to the classical tradition's approach to feminist questions. And, of course, these must go without saying. Because if Jones's own position – and that of the classical tradition – are themselves gendered, then Jones fails to offer a gender-neutral much less gender-free account of gender. Gender, it seems, has no place in IR theory – *not* because it is 'unbalanced' and therefore out of bounds, but because it is something we see the world through and therefore no 'home' can hold it.

Suggestions for further thinking

Topic 1 Feminism

The best way to get a sense of what feminism is and the impact it has had on IR theory and international politics is to read feminist IR theorists themselves. This approach also helps readers to stay focused on feminist questions about international politics rather than on disciplinary IR questions about feminism of the sort someone like Jones asks of feminism (Zalewski, 1995). Elshtain's *Woman and War* and Enloe's *Bananas, Beaches, and Bases* are the traditional starting points for an encounter with feminist IR theory. Accessibly written and full of illustrations, they provide lively introductions into the literature, as do a number of books that either look to IR theory most specifically (Tickner, 1992; Sylvester, 1994) or provide collections of feminist IR writings (Grant and Newland (eds), 1991; Peterson (ed.), 1992)

Suggested reading

Marysia Zalewski (1995) 'Well, What is the Feminist Perspective on Bosnia?' *International Affairs* 71(2):339–56.

Jean Bethke Elshtain (1987) *Women and War*. New York: Basic Books.

Cynthia Enloe (1989) *Bananas, Beaches and Bases: Making Feminist Sense of International Politics*. Berkeley: University of California Press.

J. Ann Tickner (1992) *Gender in International Relations: Feminist Perspectives on achieving Global Security*. New York: Columbia University Press.

Christine Sylvester (1994) *Feminist Theory and International Relations in a Postmodern Era*. Cambridge: Cambridge University Press.

Rebecca Grant and Kathleen Newland (eds) (1991) *Gender and International Relations*. Milton Keynes: Open University Press.

V. Spike Peterson, (ed.) (1992) *Gendered States: Feminist (Re)Visions of International Relations Theory*. Boulder, Col.: Lynne Rienner.

Topic 2 Masculinity

Feminists have long argued that their concern is not only with women (although that is a central focus of their research) but on how gender (femininity *and masculinity*) construct, constrain, and empower all gendered bodies. They are no strangers to works like Connell's *Masculinities* and other classic texts of masculinity (as Carver et al., 1998, argue in their reply to Jones). Feminist IR scholars have not only argued that 'gender is not a synonym for women' (Carver, 1996). They have theoretically and empirically raised the 'man' question in international relations (Zalewski and Parpart, 1998).

Suggested reading

Robert W. Connell (1995) *Masculinities*. Cambridge: Cambridge University Press.

Terrell Carver, Molly Cochran, and Judith Squires (1998) 'Gendering Jones: Feminisms, IRs, and Masculinities', *Review of International Studies* 24(2):283–97.

Terrell Carver (1996) *Gender is Not a Synonym for Women*. Boulder, CO: Lynne Rienner.

Marysia Zalewski and Jane Parpart (eds) (1998) *The 'Man' Question in International Relations*. Boulder, Col.: Westview.

Globalization

Are we at the end of history?

It is appropriate that a book examining international relations as a site of cultural practices imbued with conscious and unconscious ideologies should close by examining a myth that claims that ideological struggles are over. This is precisely what Francis Fukuyama claims in his famous 1989 essay 'The End of History?' and later elaborates on in his book *The End of History and the Last Man* (1992). Fukuyama argues that liberal democracy as a system of governance has won an 'unabashed victory' over other ideas to the point that liberalism is the only legitimate ideology left in the world. Not only are there no coherent ideological challengers to liberalism, liberalism itself is free of irrational internal contradictions which lead to the collapse of ideologies. Having no internal contradictions means that liberalism is a finished idea. For Fukuyama, all this marks 'the end point of mankind's ideological evolution' and means that liberalism is 'the final form of human government' (1989:271). Because the history of the conflict of ideas in the form of ideological struggle is now over, all that remains to be done is to spread liberal ideology throughout the world as a material way of life, through social, political, and economic institutions.

Fukuyama's argument could not have been more timely. Published the summer before the Berlin Wall came down, Fukuyama's essay appeared to have predicted the thawing Cold War's final melting, a melting made possible by the absence of any credible rivals to liberalism. The supposed predictive power of Fukuyama's myth was not the only thing that made it popular with IR scholars. If Fukuyama had predicted the end of the Cold War, mainstream IR scholars surely had not. Left bewildered and embarrassed, they looked around for something meaningful to say. Debating the insecurities of anarchy (Chapters 2, 3, and 4), for example, just wasn't as gripping as it used to be, now that the US was considered by most to be the uncontested global hegemon and world police officer (Brielmyer). IR scholars and their traditional theories were beginning to look obsolete. But, thankfully, Fukuyama's myth not only foretold the death of the classical Cold War strategic paradigm, it made possible an entirely new realm of research – the study of 'globalization'.

Globalization has become the trendiest craze in IR theory at the turn of the century. What is globalization? That's a good question, and one that scholars in and out of IR have had difficulty grappling with. Globalization has been described as 'a term which can refer to anything from the Internet to a hamburger' (Strange, 1996:xiii). That's because theorists disagree on just about everything regarding 'globalization'. They disagree about when 'globalization' started. Some date its beginning after WWII (Leyshon, 1997:133), while others argue it is as old as capitalism itself (Hirst and Thompson, 1996:2). They disagree about what it expresses (economic, geographic, social, political, or cultural phenomena) and whether or not one or more of these phenomena should be emphasized over the others. And they disagree about whether 'globalization' is a process, an ideology ('globalism') or a 'state of being' ('globality') (Marchand, 2000:219). Given all these disagreements, it is not surprising that one theorist described 'globalization' as simply 'a floating sign of many different problematics' (Ó Tuathail, 1998:85).

Among these many problematics, two stand out. They are two traditions of international political economy – (neo)liberalism and historical materialism and their expressions of globalization (Table 6.1). (Neo)liberal expressions of globalization are based on classical liberal economic arguments that see international economic

Table 6.1 (Neo)liberal and historical materialist takes on globalization

	(Neo)liberal	Historical Materialist
Nature of international economic relations	Harmonious	Conflictual
Distribution of economic goods	All who participate in economic processes benefit	Capitalist economic processes redistribute wealth so that the rich get richer and the poor get poorer
Relationship between politics and economics	Economics *should* drive politics. Why? Because harmonious, beneficial economic processes can 'spill over' and create harmonious, beneficial political processes like democracy within and among sovereign nation-states	Economics *does* drive politics. Because economic processes are conflictual, this means that political processes are conflictual within and among sovereign nation-states
Take on globalization	Globalization is good because it spreads the economic, political, and cultural benefits of liberalism	Globalization is bad because it does not result in an equitable distribution of global wealth
Globalization's place in history	It is the 'end of history'	It is the capitalist stage of history. History ends at the next stage, when socialism or communism is realized.

processes as harmonious realms in which economic exchange processes like free trade spread wealth and increase the quality of life for all who participate. And not only does economics bring economic benefits, it brings political benefits as well, primarily through the spread of liberal democratic institutions in which liberty, freedom, and justice for all are to be guaranteed because the people hold political power. This is why classical liberals believe that economic processes should drive political processes.

In an era of 'globalization', classical liberal principles become (neo)liberal expressions of 'globalization', in which three processes occur simultaneously and for the good of humankind – economic liberalization (like free trade), political democratization (power to the people), and cultural universalization (some would say the 'Americanization' of the globe; see Strange, 1996). For (neo)liberals, 'globalization' is about the benevolent spread of liberal economic, political, and cultural processes, institutions, and practices throughout the world.

In contrast, historical materialist expressions of 'globalization' have their roots in classical Marxism. For historical materialists, economic processes drive political and cultural processes. Unlike (neo)liberals, historical materialists regard international economic processes as being conflictual, primarily between economic classes (owners and workers). These conflicts among economic classes are what lead to historical changes in institutions, ideas, and everyday life. History, therefore, is the history of the class struggle (as Marx put it), and history will not end until the class struggle ends. That can only happen when capitalism (our current global economic system) is transcended by communist economic, political, and cultural processes.

Historical materialists generally agree with (neo)liberals that 'globalization' is a process, ideology, and/or way of living that spreads capitalist ideas, institutions, and practices throughout the world. But historical materialists strongly disagree with (neo)liberals on two important points. First, unlike (neo)liberals, they believe that capitalist economics and liberal ideology are themselves premised on contradictions. They are not the final, complete expressions of economics and politics that someone like Fukuyama claims they are because economic classes are still at odds with one another. Second, according to historical materialists, this means that liberalism is not the final stage of history. It is not 'the end of history'. Rather, it is a step on the way to communism, the real end of history. As these criticisms make clear, historical materialists don't disagree with Fukuyama that history will have an end. They simply disagree with his claim that liberalism is 'the end of history'.

(Neo)liberal expressions of globalization are by far the most influential in IR theory and in policy circles. They seem to be the most 'historically accurate' in the wake of the post-Cold War collapse of socialist and communist states and ideologies. They clearly complement post-Cold War theories of neoidealism (Chapter 3). And they inform policies that create regional free trade organizations like the European Union and the North American Free Trade Agreement (NAFTA) and that effect 'global' institutions like the World Trade Organization.

There are lots of problems with (neo)liberal and historical materialist expressions of 'globalization', but this is not the place to debate the shortcomings and merits of each (see Herod et al., eds, 1998). Instead, my interest lies in what these debates and disagreements about 'globalization' have to do with Fukuyama's myth 'it is the end of history'. *Fukuyama's myth cleared the ideological ground for (neo)liberal expressions of globalization to go virtually uncontested.* By arguing that the history of ideological struggle was over and liberalism had won, Fukuyama put liberalism itself beyond debate in two important ways. First, because liberalism had 'won' out over ideological challengers, this meant that any critiques of liberalism from 'old leftist' ideological traditions like socialism and communism (as well as from the 'old right' of fascism) were regarded as outdated and need not be taken seriously by IR scholars. Second, because liberalism was presented in Fukuyama's work as a finished ideology, scholarly attention should be directed away from analysis focused on possible contradictions *within* liberalism and towards analysis of the global spread of (neo)liberal processes, institutions, and practices that follow from the 'globalization' of liberal ideology.

In this chapter, I will explore how Fukuyama's myth 'it is the end of history' makes liberalism the global stage on which international politics in an era of 'globalization' unfolds. By Fukuyama's own account, for his myth to function, liberalism must be a finished ideology with no credible external rivals. In other words, liberalism must be free of contradictions, both internally and externally. Fukuyama makes the case that liberalism has no credible external ideological threats. But, in directing our attention towards the ideological challengers of liberalism, Fukuyama deflects our attention away from liberalism's own internal contradiction – the contradiction between its creation of boundless desires within individuals for the good life and its failure to fully satisfy or control these desires. It is only by substituting economic consumption for personal satisfaction that liberalism defers and displaces individual encounters with what Fukuyama admits is 'the empty core of liberalism' (1989:281) – its inability to deliver a meaningful life.

We see these processes of endless substitution, displacement, and deferral acted out in the 1998 film *The Truman Show*. Not only is Truman Burbank, the 'on the air, unaware' star of a television programme 'The Truman Show', offered a utopian world in which his material desires are met as a way to control his personal desires and keep him on the set that is his hometown of Seahaven. So, too, are Truman's post-historical viewers offered substitutes for their desires. In place of their desire for history, they are offered 'The Truman Show' – a place where history as an ideological struggle between good (Truman) and evil (the show's producer Christof) is staged for them.

But when Truman escapes Seahaven and 'The Truman Show' ends, post-historical liberalism's ability to displace individual desires for history on to 'The Truman Show' no longer functions. And this makes us wonder if Fukuyama's promise that liberalism's post-Cold War 'triumph' over ideological challengers means we are at 'the end of history'. For, if we accept Fukuyama's argument, liberalism may have dealt with ideological challengers. But, as *The Truman Show* suggests, it has not (and I would suggest, it cannot) resolved its own internal contradiction between creating and fulfilling desires, desires that propel Truman out of history and possibly lead his viewers back into history.

To make sense of all of this, we need to examine Fukuyama's claim 'it is the end of history'. I will do this by focusing on three questions: (1) What does Fukuyama mean by the end of history? (2) What does liberalism as a post-historical ideology look like to Fukuyama? (3) How does Fukuyama appear to resolve liberalism's internal tension between creating unfulfillable desires and attempting to fulfil them so that his myth 'it is the end of history' appears to be true?

What does the myth say?

In his essay 'The End of History?', Fukuyama begins by reflecting that 'something very fundamental has happened in world history' and this something is usually described as post-Cold War peace 'breaking out in many regions of the world' (1989:270). But Fukuyama laments that analyses of the end of the Cold War tend to be 'superficial' because they lack a 'conceptual framework for distinguishing between what is essential and what is contingent or accidental in world history' (1989:270). Fukuyama takes as his task to investigate 'a process that gives coherence and order to the daily headlines' and, he claims, this process is 'an unabashed victory of economic and political liberalism' (1989:270).

As Fukuyama puts it, 'What we may be witnessing is not just the end of the Cold War, or the passing of a particular period of post-war history, but *the end of history as such*: that is, the end point of mankind's ideological evolution and the universalization of Western liberal democracy as the final form of human government' (1989:271; my italics). But while the 'victory of liberalism' is an ideological victory – in that no other ideas or ideologies pose a challenge to it – its victory 'is as yet incomplete in the real or material world' (1989:271). That is why we don't see every state in the world practising liberal political and economic principles. But Fukuyama argues that 'there are powerful reasons for believing that it is the ideal that will govern the material world *in the long run* (1989:271; italics in the original). In other words, it is only a matter of time before liberalism is 'globalized' as both an unchallenged ideology and as a material way of life.

How does Fukuyama make his argument? He does so by privileging a particular way of understanding history. History, for Fukuyama, is 'a dialectical process with a beginning, a middle, and an end' (1989:271). A dialectical process is a process though which the contradiction between a dominant truth (thesis) and its opposite (antithesis) are reconciled to produce a higher truth (synthesis). This higher truth or synthesis becomes the new thesis, which will necessarily be opposed by a new antithesis. This process continues until 'all prior contradictions are resolved and all human needs are satisfied' (1989:272). From this point onward, 'there is no struggle or conflict over "large" issues . . . ; what remains is primarily economic activity' (1989:272). And when we reach this point, history is over.

This way of describing history draws upon Hegel's notion of dialectical history (see Figure 6.1). For Hegel, 'history culminated in an absolute moment – a moment in which a final, rational form of society and state became victorious' (Fukuyama, 1989:271). For Hegel, this moment arrived in 1806, when, after the French Revolution, 'the basic *principles* of the liberal democratic state could not be improved upon' (1989:272). Now, as then, liberalism's 'theoretical truth is absolute and could not be improved upon' (1989:274). All that remains to be done is to spatially extend liberal principles throughout the world (1989:272).

Many of us are familiar with this Hegelian way of thinking about history because Karl Marx borrowed Hegel's dialectic to make his argument about how contradictions among economic classes would 'drag history ahead' and culminate

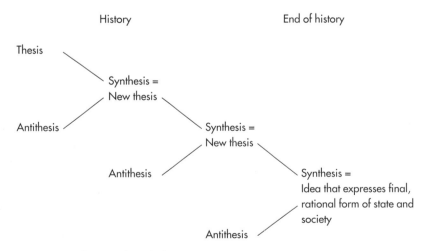

Figure 6.1 The Hegelian dialectic

with the realization of communism. Marx was interested in material economic forces of history. But this isn't the way Hegel thought about dialectics. Hegel, in contrast to Marx, was interested not in the progress of material well-being first and foremost but in the progress of the idea. In Hegel's dialectic, it is not economic classes that are in conflict; it is ideologies that are in conflict (see Table 6.2). For Hegel, ideology or consciousness about the world is what causes the world to change materially. As Fukuyama puts it, 'consciousness will ultimately remake the material world in its own image' (1989:274).

For Fukuyama, ideological consciousness is 'the real subject underlying the apparent jumble of current events in the history of ideology' (1989:273). In other words, it is the triumph of liberalism that made the end of the Cold War possible, and not, for example, the economic collapse of the former Soviet Union that made liberal consciousness possible. Yes, modern free market economics underwrites and helps to stabilize this liberal consciousness. And so Fukuyama claims the end of history is marked by 'the universal homogenous state as liberal democracy in the political sphere combined with easy access to VCRs and stereos in the economic' (1989:275). But underwriting and stabilizing should not be confused with causing something to happen. For Fukuyama, as for Hegel, ideological consciousness – not economic materiality – is the cause of change, not its effect (1989:273).

How can Fukuyama argue that liberalism's 'theoretical truth is absolute and could not be improved upon' (1989:274) to the point that we are now at the end of history? He does so by posing a question: 'Are there . . . any fundamental "contradictions" in human life that cannot be resolved in the context of modern liberalism, that would be resolvable by an alternative political-economic structure?' (1989:275). His answer is no.

Fukuyama gets to this answer by considering the historical status of ideological challengers to liberalism in the twentieth century – fascism and communism (see Table 6.3). He argues that 'fascism was destroyed as a living ideology by World War II. This defeat,' he concedes, 'of course, was on a very material level, but it amounted to a defeat of the idea as well' because no ideological movements based on fascism have survived long in the post-war era (1989:275). Communism's challenge to liberalism, Fukuyama argues, 'was far more serious' (1989:275). Communism claimed that liberalism could not resolve its own internal contradiction between capital and labour, between the owning class and the working class (1989:275). Fukuyama claims that 'classless society' has been achieved in the United States. By this, he does not mean that the gap between the rich and the poor is not growing, but that 'the root causes of economic inequalities do not have to do with the underlying legal and social structure of our [US] society' (1989:275–6). As a result, 'the appeal of communism in

Table 6.2 Hegelian and Marxist understandings of history

	Hegel	*Marx*
Understanding of history	Dialectical	Dialectical
Nature of dialectic	Idealist	Materialist
What clashes in the dialectic?	Ideologies	Economic classes

Table 6.3 Ideological challengers to liberalism

	Critique of liberalism	Why challenge fails
Fascism	Political weakness, materialism, anomie, and lack of community of West = fundamental contradictions in liberal society	Destroyed as a living ideology both materially and ideologically by WWII
Communism	Liberal contradiction between capital and labour/owner and workers cannot be resolved	• state commitments to communism in China and the Soviet Union only rhetorical • bourgeois consumerism embraced internationally • no state offers genuine communist alternative to liberalism
Religion	Liberal consumerism means core liberalism is hollow, meaningless	Offers no universalizable political alternative to liberalism
Nationalism	Offers no generalizable critique of liberalism. Only critical of some particular expressions of liberalism through specific non-representative governments	Because it has no generalizable critique of liberalism, nationalism is not necessarily incompatible with liberal ideology

the developed Western world . . . is lower today than any time since the end of the First World War' (1989:276).

But what about the rest of the world? To make the argument that liberal consciousness pervades the West tells us nothing new. And Fukuyama recognizes this, arguing that 'it is precisely in the non-European world that one is most struck by the occurrence of major ideological transformations' (1989:276). He cites the example of Japan, a country that had liberal political and economic principles imposed on it after WWII. What is important in the Japanese case, according to Fukuyama, is 'that the essential elements of economic and political liberalism have been so successfully grafted onto uniquely Japanese traditions and institutions,' thus ensuring their long-term survival (1989:276). In the case of the Newly Industrialized Countries in Asia (NICs), the evidence is even more compelling because 'political liberalism has been following economic liberalism' as a result of 'the victory of the idea of the universal homogenous state' and not due to external imposition as in the case of Japan (1989:277).

Fukuyama even manages to cite communist China as an example of the triumph of liberalism because 'Marxism and ideological principle have become virtually irrelevant as guides to policy, and . . . bourgeois consumerism has a real meaning in that country for the first time since the revolution' (1989:278). As a result, 'China can no longer act as a beacon for illiberal forces around the world' (1989:278).

But, of course, 'it is the developments in the Soviet Union – the original "homeland of the world proletariat" – that have put the final nail in the coffin of the Marxist-Leninist alternative to liberal democracy' (1989:278). The demise of the Soviet Union seals the triumph of liberalism for Fukuyama. As he puts it, since

Gorbachev came to power there has been 'a revolutionary assault on the most fundamental institutions and principles of Stalinism, and their replacement by other principles which do not amount to liberalism *per se* but whose only connecting thread is liberalism' (italics in the original; 1989:279). And so communism joins fascism as a 'dead' ideology. This does not mean that Fukuyama would describe the former Soviet Union as liberal or democratic, and he is clear that this is beside the point. For 'at the end of history it is not necessary that all societies become successful liberal societies, merely that they end their ideological pretensions of representing different and higher forms of human society' (1989:280).

Concluding that fascism and communism are dead, Fukuyama looks round for alternative ideologies that might challenge liberalism in the future. He identifies two – religion and nationalism (see Table 6.3). Of religious fundamentalism, Fukuyama contends that while this may well be a response to 'the emptiness at the core of liberalism', it is unlikely to represent a political response. 'Only Islam has offered a theocratic state as a political alternative to both liberalism and communism', but because this has little appeal for non-Muslims, Fukuyama argues it lacks 'universal significance' (1989:281). Nationalism, on the other hand, does not represent a clear 'irreconcilable contradiction in the heart of liberalism' (1989:281). And because nationalism is generally an ideology about independence from another group, people, or state, Fukuyama concludes that it does 'not offer anything like a comprehensive agenda for socio-economic organization' (1989:281–2).

Having considered the ideologies past and future that could challenge liberalism, Fukuyama concludes that 'the present world seems to confirm that the fundamental principles of socio-political organization have not advanced terribly far since 1806' (1989:282). That doesn't rule out the possibility of some 'new ideology or previously unrecognized contradictions in liberal societies' to challenge liberalism, but none was apparent to Fukuyama at the time he wrote his essay (1989:282).

Assuming we have reached 'the end of history', Fukuyama asks what all this means for international relations. What will international politics look like in a 'de-ideologized world'? (1989:282). 'The end of history' does not mark the end of material conflicts, only ideological conflicts. Conflicts will still rage in 'the vast bulk of the Third World [which] remains very much mired in history' (1989:282). But 'international life for the part of the world that has reached the end of history is far more preoccupied with economics than with politics or strategy' (1989:283). And so in the de-ideologized world, 'we are far more likely to see the "Common Marketization" of world politics' than we are to see the resurgence of large-scale conflict among sovereign nation-states, 'international anarchy' notwithstanding (1989:284). This does not mean there will be no conflict among sovereign nation-states. This is likely between 'historical states' and 'post-historical states' (1989:285). Nor does this mean that Marxist-Leninism won't try to stage an ideological comeback, but, as far as Fukuyama is concerned, it 'is dead as a mobilizing ideology' and so presents little threat for dragging us back into history (1989:285).

Overall, Fukuyama concludes that 'the end of history' will be rather boring. If ideological struggles made us live risky, purposeful lives that called for 'daring, courage, imagination, and idealism', the 'de-ideological' age of post-history will be marked by 'economic calculation, the endless solving of technical problems, environmental concerns, and the satisfaction of sophisticated consumer demands'

(1989:285–6). It will be 'just the perpetual caretaking of the museum of human history' (1989:286). All this seems to depress Fukuyama, for he writes, 'I can feel in myself, and see in others around me, a powerful nostalgia for the time when history existed' (1989:286). And he concludes by wondering if 'centuries of boredom at the end of history will serve to get history started once again' (1989:286). But, if it does, then Fukuyama cannot claim that liberalism's post-Cold War 'triumph' over all ideological challenges marks the end of history.

It is easy to see how Fukuyama's description of the post-Cold War era as 'de-ideological', low-conflict, and post-historical set the stage for neoliberal expressions of globalization to become the 'next big thing' in IR theory. Since ideological struggles, much less large-scale political conflict, were now a thing of the past, all that remained to be done was to explore the many ways in which liberalism was being spread worldwide in economic, political, and cultural forms. Or was there?

Fukuyama supports his myth 'it is the end of history' by making the case that there are no 'living' ideological challengers to liberalism. While the 'facts' of Fukuyama's case have received a lot of attention and are hotly debated, what goes without saying in Fukuyama's myth is that liberalism itself is free of internal contradictions. Fukuyama simply asserts this and leaves it up to fully expressed, coherent ideological rivals to make the case that he is wrong. Instead, he makes the case that they are wrong.

But what happens if we look *inside* liberalism? What if we ignore the challenges posed by 'alternative ideologies' like fascism, communism, religious fundamentalism, and nationalism and simply focus our attention on what makes liberalism itself function? If we do so our attention is drawn away from liberalism's would-be challengers to that unresolvable tension within liberalism – its creation of unfulfillable desires that (by definition) it can only fail to fulfil. By Fukuyama's own admission, for his myth 'it is the end of history' to function, liberalism must be free not only of external challengers but of internal contradictions as well. But liberalism's relationship to the creation and fulfilment of desires always threatens to unravel not only its promises for the good life but Fukuyama's claim that 'it is the end of history'.

This tension is exquisitely explored in *The Truman Show*. The film is set in a post-historical era, in which economic concerns and cultural nostalgia have replaced political and ideological struggles. What makes this post-historical world function is the success of the television programme 'The Truman Show' in staging history for its viewers and substituting viewers' desires for historical and ideological engagement with their consumption of 'The Truman Show'. But when Truman reaches his 'end of history' by escaping Seahaven, his viewers are left with empty airtime that might represent 'the empty core of liberalism' (1989:281). And we may wonder if the ending of 'The Truman Show' also marks the end of Fukuyama's myth 'it is the end of history'.

The Truman Show

How's it gonna end? That is the question that grips viewers of the 1998 film *The Truman Show* – not for the usual reasons about cinematic climaxes and suspense but because the film *The Truman Show* is about a television programme called

'The Truman Show'. Nothing terribly strange about that. But there is a twist. Truman Burbank/Jim Carrey, the star of 'The Truman Show', is the only person in the world who does not know that 'The Truman Show' is a television show and that Seahaven Island where he has lived his entire life is an elaborate television set. And one day he is bound to find out. When he does, 'The Truman Show' (at least in its current form) will end.

How could anyone be so duped about the 'reality' of his life? Easily! As Christof/Ed Harris, the 'creator' of 'The Truman Show' tells us in an interview, 'We accept the reality of the world with which we're presented. It's as simple as that.' And for Truman Burbank, 'The Truman Show' is the only reality he has ever known. From before his birth, Truman has been on television. His whole life – from the exciting to the mundane – has been recorded by hidden cameras (about 5,000 cameras to be exact) and transmitted non-stop worldwide as 'The Truman Show'. First placed in Truman's birth-mother's womb, cameras were later hidden throughout Seahaven – not only in streets and houses but also in buttons, vending machines, a pencil sharpener, and even Seahaven's moon. By the time we meet the 30-year-old Truman, the entire island of Seahaven has been built as a television stage housed in an

Plate 6.1 Truman captured by a 'bathroom cam' as he draws on the mirror and makes silly faces.
© Paramount Pictures, courtesy of The Ronald Grant Archive

enormous dome, including a complete town, sea, and sky. Seahaven is so big, the film tells us, that apart from the Great Wall of China, it is the only unnatural object visible from outer space.

Not only is Truman's 'natural' environment unnatural, so too is his social environment. Everyone on the show has been cast into their roles, including Truman's mother, wife, best friend, and an entire town of neighbours, acquaintances, and strangers who inhabit Seahaven. The television viewing audience knows that all of the people in Seahaven are playing roles in 'The Truman Show' – all of them but Truman himself. But for Truman, he and everyone he meets and everything he encounters are real. The woman cast as Truman's mother, for example, is the only mother Truman has ever known. Truman does not know that he was the product of an unwanted pregnancy and that his birth coincided with a pre-set airtime for 'The Truman Show', making him the child selected as its star. Nor does Truman know that he is the first person in the world to have been legally adopted by a corporation – the corporation that broadcasts 'The Truman Show'.

Why go to these lengths to produce a television show? As Christof explains, 'We've become bored with watching actors give us phoney emotions. We're tired of pyrotechnics and special effects. While the world he inhabits is in some respects counterfeit, there's nothing fake about Truman himself. No scripts, no cue cards. . . . It isn't always Shakespeare but it's genuine. It's a life'.

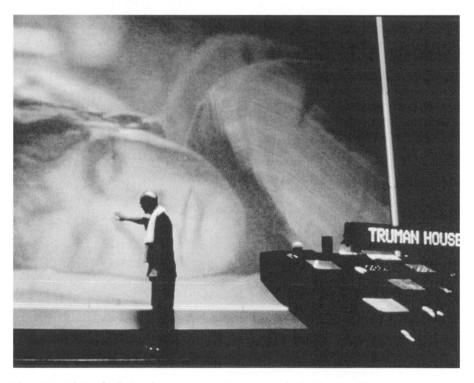

Plate 6.2 Christof admires his creations – Truman and 'The Truman Show'.
© Paramount Pictures, courtesy of The Ronald Grant Archive

And watching Truman's life has glued viewers to their television sets for 30 years. As we learn from the television programme 'TruTalk', a 'forum for issues growing out of the show', 'One point seven billion were there for his birth. Two-hundred twenty countries tuned in for his first steps.' 'The Truman Show' is a truly global phenomenon.

To emphasize the impact 'The Truman Show' has on its viewing public, the film cuts back and forth between action on 'The Truman Show' and scenes of its viewing public. We see viewers in the busy Truman Bar, a theme bar packed with 'Truman Show' paraphernalia and dotted with televisions that broadcast only 'The Truman Show'. We see two elderly women clutching pillows with Truman's grinning face on them engrossed in an episode of the show. We see a man who seems to do nothing but watch 'The Truman Show' while lying in his bathtub. And we see two parking attendants glued to 'The Truman Show' throughout their shifts.

Why is 'The Truman Show' so popular? What are audiences looking for in 'The Truman Show', and what do they find?

Christof tells us that viewers find not only an escape from boredom but 'the way the world should be'. This – Seahaven – is the world Christof has created for Truman. Seahaven is nostalgically modelled after a 1950s American television show. Not only do the costumes and sets have a fifties feel to them, but everyone on set seems to have a fifties attitude. In this economically prosperous community, everyone is friendly and caring towards their neighbour, family life is stable, and crime is at a minimum if it exists at all. Seahaven, then, is a slice of the past made present. And because Truman lives his real life in Seahaven – his only real world – Seahaven is a living museum. Never dead or static, Seahaven is where the action is, even if that action is the tedious daily routines of an insurance salesperson. Seahaven is where living history takes place. Tuning into 'The Truman Show' is like turning on history.

Seahaven is where living history takes place not primarily because it is stylistically and attitudinally a throwback to the 1950s. As in Fukuyama's explanation of history, Seahaven is a site of living history because it is a site of ideological struggle. This ideological struggle is between Truman and Christof. It is the final ideological struggle between liberalism and some form of totalitarian ideology (like communism or fascism). Truman represents liberalism; Christof, totalitarianism.

Why is such a struggle necessary in the idyllic world of Seahaven? To put it differently, what could Truman possibly want that he cannot have in Seahaven? The simple answer is freedom. Once Truman realizes he is living in a controlled environment, he does what Fukuyama says one must do when in the grips of ideological struggle. He breaks out of his own boring daily routines and lives a risky, purposeful life that calls for 'daring, courage, imagination, and idealism' (Fukuyama, 1989:285–6). But how does Truman get to the point where he wants his freedom more than he wants the world of Seahaven in which Christof claims all of Truman's needs are met? Truman gets there because not all of his desires are met.

Christof admits that Truman's desire to explore the world around him had to be controlled, for if Truman left the set, the show would be over. As Christof puts it, 'As Truman grew up, we were forced to manufacture ways to keep him on the island.' And so Christof offers Truman a loving family, a secure job, and a friendly place to live in rather than a life of adventure beyond Seahaven. Whenever Truman expresses a desire to leave Seahaven, this substitution of stability for adventure is

Plate 6.3 Truman nostalgically looks at the family photo album.
© Paramount Pictures, courtesy of The Ronald Grant Archive

activated. Truman's mother shows him family albums and has him watch the
television programme 'Show me the Way to go Home', which celebrates the small-
town values of a place like Seahaven and which emotionally manipulates Truman to
stay where he is.

But the struggle to control Truman's desire has not always been so easy. This
is best illustrated in the film in a flashback in which Truman the college student falls
for an 'extra', Lauren, which complicates Christof's plans to have Truman marry
Meryl, the character Christof has cast to be Truman's future wife.

Truman: I'm Truman.
Lauren: Yeah. I know. Look, Truman, I'm not allowed to talk to you. You know.
[Truman notices that Lauren is wearing a pin that says 'How's it gonna end?']
Truman: I like your pin. Was wondering that myself.
Lauren: Mm.
Truman: Would you wanna maybe, possibly . . . sometime go out for some pizza or
 something? Friday? Saturday? Sunday? Monday? Tuesday? . . .
[Lauren writes on a notepad 'NOW'.]
Lauren: If we don't go now, it won't happen. Do you understand? So what are you
 gonna do?
[The cameras lose them for a while as they sneak out of the library. The cameras
discover them going to the beach together. Cut to the beach.]
Lauren: We have so little time. They're going to be here any minute.
Truman: Who are they?

Lauren: They don't want me talking to you.

Truman: Then don't talk.

[Truman kisses Lauren. A car speeds onto the beach.]

Lauren: They're here. Truman.

Truman: What do they want?

Lauren: Listen to me. Everyone knows about . . . everyone knows everything you do. 'Cause they're pretending, Truman. Do you. . . . Do you understand? Everybody's pretending.

Truman [looking perplexed]:   Lauren.

Lauren: No, no, no, ah, my name's not Lauren. No, no. My name's Sylvia.

Truman [confused]:   Sylvia?

[A man gets out of the car claiming to be Lauren's father.]

Lauren: He's lying! Truman, please! Don't listen to him! Everything I've told you is the truth! . . . This . . . it – it's fake. It's all for you.

Truman: I don't understand.

Lauren: And . . . and the sky and the sea, everything. It's a set. It's a show.

[Father intervenes.]

Truman: I really would like to know what's going on!

Lauren's Father: Schizophrenia. It's episodes. . . . You forget it, forget everything.

Lauren: Don't do it! Don't Truman! . . . Truman, he's lying! Get out of here. Come and find me.

But then Lauren's father tells Truman that he is moving his family to Fiji, and he and Lauren exit in the car.

Truman is left on the beach with Lauren's/Sylvia's forgotten sweater, which he keeps as a memento. In future episodes, we see Truman dreaming about Sylvia while looking at her sweater, trying to construct a composite of her face from pictures in women's magazines, and expressing his desire to go to Fiji. All of this illustrates Christof's bind. He must produce desires in Truman, like the desire for a heterosexual family, in order for the show to go on. Indeed, Christof boasts in an interview that he is determined to deliver to his viewers the first on-air conception. And in the world of Seahaven, for Truman to be involved in such a conception it must take place within the confines of a legitimate union. So Truman must marry. But what Christof cannot control is who Truman wants to marry. He wants Lauren/Sylvia.

At this point, Truman doesn't follow Sylvia off the set, in part because – despite Sylvia's attempt to enlighten him – he doesn't understand it is a set. And even if he did, Christof has instilled in Truman a fear of flying and a terror of water, the natural boundary around Seahaven Island. Truman's terror of water was 'produced' in the 'episode' in which Truman's father was drowned in a sailing accident for which Truman feels responsible. Not only does this make Truman give up sailing. He won't take a ferry across the bay nor will he even drive his car across the bridge.

So what is Christof to do with Truman's desire for Sylvia? Displace it, of course. Immediately after Lauren's/Sylvia's exit from the show, Truman's mother is scripted with an illness, and Truman must remain in Seahaven to care for her. And in place of Lauren/Sylvia, Christof gives Truman Meryl, whom Truman is encouraged to marry on the rebound.

What does all of this tell us about the worlds of 'The Truman Show' and *The Truman Show*? How do they make sense of their worlds, and what do they say is typical and deviant in those worlds? It is important to ask these questions for both the television problem 'The Truman Show' and for the film *The Truman Show* because the ability of each world to function is related to the smooth function of the other.

Let's start by answering these questions for the television programme 'The Truman Show'. 'The Truman Show' makes sense of the world by celebrating history. While on the surface the show's celebration of history is stylistically and attitudinally nostalgic, more fundamentally the show's celebration of history is ideological. Or, to combine the two, 'The Truman Show' is nostalgic for ideology. It celebrates the ideological struggle between good and evil, between an 'on the air, unaware' Truman and his creator and controller Christof. Truman and Christof represent different ideological positions. Truman represents the desire for freedom and the right to make choices for his own life (a desire for liberalism fully expressed), and Christof represents the desire to maintain totalitarian control over Truman's life and world. Truman's and Christof's ideological positions are locked in a dialectical contradiction (see Figure 6.2).

What is typical in the world of 'The Truman Show' is Truman remaining blissfully ignorant of his situation. A typical day is one in which Truman has yet to awaken to the ideological struggle for his freedom from Christof that awaits him. Such typical days are produced by Christof by containing Truman's desires within the utopian world of Seahaven, usually by substituting the category of what Truman wants (a wife and a loving marriage, for example) for the specific thing/person he wants (Lauren/Sylvia). So Truman gets a wife, for example, but that wife is Meryl, not Sylvia.

What is deviant in the world of 'The Truman Show' is Truman becoming ideologically aware and ultimately exiting his prison, thereby exiting history. What leads to Truman's ideological awakening is Christof's inability to fulfil Truman's desires. Loyal viewers (who seem to be everyone outside of Seahaven) know that

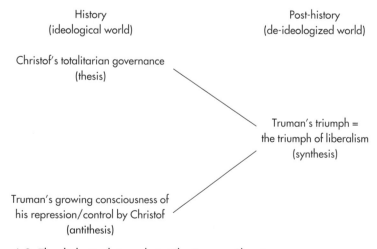

Figure 6.2 The dialectical struggle in 'The Truman Show'

Table 6.4 What is typical and deviant in the historical world of the television programme 'The Truman Show'?

Typical	Truman is unaware of his ideological struggle with Christof because his desires are contained within the utopian world of Seahaven
Deviant	Compelled by unfulfilled desires, Truman becomes ideologically aware and frees himself from Christof and from Seahaven

Truman's ideological awakening is imminent. Knowing this, they know the answer to the question 'How's it gonna end?' 'The Truman Show' ends with Truman's 'unabashed victory' over Christof's totalitarianism, a victory driven by Truman's unfulfilled desires (Table 6.4).

What about *The Truman Show*? How does it make sense of the world? What does it say is typical and deviant in that world? To answer these questions, we must look beyond the world of the television programme 'The Truman Show' and think about the relationship in the film between the television programme and those who watch it. If 'The Truman Show' the television programme represents a nostalgia for ideology and is therefore the place where history takes place, what does this tell us about how the viewers of 'The Truman Show' are positioned historically? It tells us that they are positioned in a post-historical, de-ideological era. And, as Fukuyama tells us, that must mean these viewers live in a world in which liberal capitalist ideology has triumphed over all challengers.

Think about it. We never see any conflict – ideological or otherwise – in the world beyond 'The Truman Show' that isn't about 'The Truman Show' itself. The only mention of politics and political struggle occurs when Sylvia (Truman's true love) phones into the programme 'TruTalk' to berate Christof for his imprisonment of Truman. Beyond that, there is no politics in the film. It is 'The Truman Show' that creates any sense of politics for its viewers as nothing else in the film can or does.

If the world beyond Seahaven is the world of post-history – free of ideological struggle and politics as they would be understood in a historical world – then this post-historical world is also a de-ideological world, a place where desire cannot trouble in the ways that Truman's desire troubles and ultimately ends his ideological world. Put differently, there are no internal contradictions within the post-historical, de-ideological world of the viewers that cannot be resolved from within liberal capitalism. From the point of view of someone like Fukuyama, this is because the viewers of 'The Truman Show' are free, whereas Truman is a prisoner.

That does not mean that we don't see the viewers of 'The Truman Show' express desire all the time. They do, and they do so in relation to the television programme. In addition to expressing their desire for the world of 'The Truman Show' by watching it, viewers of 'The Truman Show' literally buy it. Everything on the show is for sale – not just the products the cast use (which are plugged in the show through product placement advertisements) but the clothes they wear and the homes they live in. All this can be ordered from the Truman catalogue. For the viewers of 'The Truman Show', Truman is not just a character in a television programme. Truman – or should we call him 'Tru(e)man'? – is a commodity. Like any commodity, he can be consumed. Consuming Truman seems to make his viewers happy.

Plate 6.4 Meryl does a product advertisement, holding up a 'Chef's Pal' knife.
© Paramount Pictures, courtesy of The Ronald Grant Archive

Like Truman's desires, then, the desires of the viewing audience of the show are encapsulated within the confines of the world of Seahaven. So long as these post-historical viewers have an outlet for their 'politics' and their 'desires' – the ideologically nostalgic space of Seahaven and the economic ability to substitute the political ideology of 'The Truman Show' with economic products from 'The Truman Show' – then their desires for history as the history of ideological struggle are met.

This is what is typical in the cinematic world of *The Truman Show* – for the televisual actions of 'The Truman Show' to fill any nostalgic longings the viewers have for politics and ideology through their daily practices of consumption (either by watching 'The Truman Show' or by purchasing products from it). Like Truman's world in which desires are satisfied with substitutes (families, fiancées, friends), the world of this viewing audience has their desires for history and ideology satisfied with consumable substitutes (viewing time and show memorabilia). What is deviant in the world of *The Truman Show* is for there to be no space – no Seahaven or Truman Burbank's life or Truman catalogue – on to which viewers can safely project their desires for history and ideology (Table 6.5).

And, of course, this is precisely where the film leaves us. When Truman exits history, his post-historical viewers are left with nowhere to project their desires for history. Certainly, they can fill the empty airtime by changing channels (as the parking attendants do in the film's final scene), but where else will they find 'real history' as the genuine struggle of a genuine character with a genuine totalitarian in control? Nowhere. As Christof told us, that is why 'The Truman Show' was staged in

Table 6.5 What is typical and deviant in the post-historical world of the film *The Truman Show*?

Typical	'The Truman Show' is the space in which its viewers consume history as the history of ideology (by watching the ideological struggle between Truman and Christof and by owning a piece of that history though the purchase of goods from 'The Truman Show')
Deviant	There is no space for viewers to safely project their desires for history and ideology because 'The Truman Show' goes off the air permanently

the first place and has had a growing audience ever since – because it is real. And that means there is no substitute for 'The Truman Show'.

All this has to make us wonder, with Truman's history over, might viewers' desire for history now be fulfilled with a return to ideological struggle – not in the form of a televisual substitute but in less apparently mediated ways? Or, to put it somewhat differently, is the end ever really the end?

Liberalism's internal contradiction, or is the end ever really the end?

The Truman Show aptly displays an unresolvable contradiction within the ideology of liberalism. Liberalism forever attempts to fulfil the desires it creates for individuals by offering them substitutes. These substitutes are often (but not always) economic. Whether this is 'the economic good life' in 'The Truman Show' or the ability to consume 'the ideological good life' for viewers of 'The Truman Show', these substitutions generally satisfy individuals for a while. But ultimately, they fail. The trick to making liberalism work – to making liberalism function – is to delay any sense of disappointment its subjects experience when economic desires fail to satisfy personal desires. Capitalism does a very good job in helping liberalism succeed on this score because the message of capitalism is that economic enjoyment can equal personal fulfilment so long as one keeps on consuming.

The Truman Show reminds us that these substitutions are not only necessary. More importantly, it reminds us that they are limited. There are limits to how happy Christof can keep Truman, no matter how hard he tries. And there are limits to how long Truman Burbank can keep his viewers satisfied. Yes, most of them cheer for his liberation from Christof. But when Truman achieves his 'unabashed victory' over Christof, where does that leave his post-historical viewers? It leaves them wallowing in the 'emptiness at the core of liberalism' (Fukuyama, 1989:281) searching for something to fill it (even if initially only by changing channels). What we don't know – and what it seems no one can control – is what form attempts to fill this empty core will take.

Leaving desires unfulfilled – whether they are for 'The Truman Show' or for something else – is a problem for liberalism. In the film, a post-'Truman Show' era is a dangerous one, for it is one in which there is no safe space on to which Truman's viewers can project their desire for something to fill the boredom of post-history and 'the empty core of liberalism' (Fukuyama, 1989:281). This is dangerous because, for liberalism to function as an ideology apparently free of internal contradictions, such a space must exist.

What does this tell us about Fukuyama's myth 'it is the end of history'? It tells us that it only appears to be true so long as liberalism's claim to be free of internal contradictions *appears to be* true. What our detour through the film *The Truman Show* tells us is that what it takes for liberalism to appear to be free of internal contradictions is the endless deferral of individual encounters with liberalism's empty core. All this suggests that, instead of writing about 'the end of history' in which liberalism is triumphant, maybe Fukuyama is writing instead about liberalism's apparent triumph – one that depends on us knowing about but never experiencing its empty core. And Fukuyama's own myth 'it is the end of history' – a myth that he evidences by directing our attention away from liberalism's internal contradiction and towards alternative ideological challenges – actually participates in liberalism's process of deferring our encounter with its empty core.

What does all of this mean for international relations in an era of 'globalization'? It means that those determined to study liberalism in a post-Cold War era might be better served by investigating not what alternative ideologies might crop up to challenge liberalism's apparent global dominance but by asking questions like, in an era of 'globalization', how will liberalism attempt to control and defer our encounter with its empty core? Or, to put it somewhat differently, how does liberalism now attempt to control our desires in ways that escape our notice?

As the protests against the World Trade Organization talks in Seattle in 1999 suggest, these are not unimportant questions. Protesters around the world (but especially in the industrialized West) offered something like a carnival of opposition to global capitalism (using art and performance art mixed with more traditional forms of demonstration), the very global capitalism that gave these protesters 'the good life'. What they objected to was not only how global capitalism's promise of the good life for some (Western industrialized states) comes at the expense of others (developing states) but also how empty is liberalism's offer of economic well-being in place of personal desire ('the empty core of liberalism'). While the former point of protest is an old Marxist complaint, the latter one requires no alternative ideological challenger to bring it into focus.

Examples like these remind us of the necessary oversights in Fukuyama's myth 'it is the end of history'. It is not just a coherent ideological challenger that can (in Fukuyama's terms) drag us back into history. It is liberalism's own internal contradiction – which makes us want total freedom but can offer us only economic freedom in its place – that creates historical and ideological struggle as well. And, even though Fukuyama chose not to focus on it when he wrote his essay in 1989, even he admits that this is a contradiction that has been at the core of liberalism from its creation.

Suggestions for further thinking

Topic 1 *Globalization*

Even though IR theorists cannot agree about what globalization is, they do agree that it is vitally important to our understanding of contemporary international life.

Globalization is not a concept that has implications only for what we consider to be the traditional international political-economy debates (between liberalism, Marxism, and mercantilism). Globalization impacts upon what we regard as the traditional domain of 'politics'. For example, IR theorists hotly debate what globalization does to the sovereign nation-state. Does the state 'wither away' in an era of globalization, or do forms of state control simply change their form? What is the role of new technologies like the internet in the processes of state control/state retreat? If the territorial state is a thing of the past because of globalization, what (if anything) is taking its place? Is the state being replaced by a truly global cosmopolitanism, for example? Or is globalization nothing more than the (not so) benevolent spread of US hegemony? These questions define the cutting edge of IR research at the beginning of the twenty-first century.

Kofman and Youngs (eds) (1996) take up these debates about the state, while Baylis and Smith (eds) (1997) situate globalization debates in relation to IR theory more generally. For an unabashed liberal defence of globalization, see Micklethwait and Wooldridge (2000). Reading this text in relation to more critical texts on globalization (Herod et al. (eds), 1998; Jameson and Miyoshi (eds), 1998; and Hay and Marsh (eds), 2000) is a good way to spark debate.

Suggested reading

Eleonore Kofman and Gillian Youngs (eds) (1996) *Globalization: Theory and Practice*. London: Pinter.

John Baylis and Steve Smith (eds) (1997) *The Globalization of World Politics*. Oxford: Oxford University Press.

Andrew Herod, Gearóid Ó Tuathail, and Susan M. Roberts (eds) (1998) *An Unruly World? Globalization, Governance, and Geography*. London: Routledge.

John Micklethwait and Adrian Wooldridge (2000) *The Future Perfect: The Challenges and Hidden Promise of Globalization*. New York: Times Press.

Fredric Jameson and Masao Miyoshi (eds) (1998) *The Cultures of Globalization*. Chapel Hill, N.C.: Duke University Press.

Colin Hay and David Marsh (eds) (2000) *Demystifying Globalization*. Boulder, Col.: St. Martin's Press.

Topic 2 The uses of history

History is another concept that we all seem to understand and accept as given. But, as Fukuyama's myth 'it is the end of history' demonstrates, even if we think we know what history *is*, we don't necessarily grasp what history or histories *do*. How does history and temporality more generally function in narrative accounts of international politics? What work does history do in IR theory? How do critical understandings of history and temporality help us to better approach IR theory? Using a text like Ermarth's (1992) as a general introduction to critical understandings of history is helpful in critically reading how classic IR theory texts (like Modelski, 1987, or Gilpin,

1983, for example) use history. Considering how history is used generally in IR theory, it is even possible to argue that IR theory debates are debates about history/temporality as much as if not more than they are about geography/spatiality, concepts that have more often occupied critical IR theorists (Weber, 1998).

Suggested reading

Elizabeth Deeds Ermarth (1992) *Sequel to History: Postmodernism and the Crisis of Representational Time*. Princeton: Princeton University Press.

George Modelski (1987) *Long Cycles in World Politics*. Seattle: University of Washington Press.

Robert Gilpin (1983) *War and Change in World Politics*. Cambridge: Cambridge University Press.

Cynthia Weber (1998) 'Reading Martin Wight's "Why is There No International Theory?" as History'. *Alternatives* 23:451–69.

Conclusion:

What does it all mean?

So far, we have concerned ourselves with how meanings are produced, mythologized, circulated, and contested in, through, and *as* culture, ideology, and IR theory. We've done this by thinking broadly about culture and ideology and then using what we have learned about these concepts to consider what makes some of the stories IR theory tells about the world appear to be true. I have called these stories IR myths, apparent truths upon which IR traditions rely in order to appear to be true. We have considered the relationships among IR theory, IR traditions, and IR myths by consulting not only classic statements in the IR literature but popular ideas about international politics and everyday life found in popular films.

This is what we have done. But why have we done it? What is at stake in this exercise of rethinking IR theory through culture, ideology, mythology, and popular film? What does it all mean?

I will address these questions by raising two more: how does IR theory make sense of the world? and what does IR theory say is typical and deviant in that world? Addressing these questions will allow me to consider how our IR myths work not only individually but together. And this will lead us to a discussion of the politics of IR theory, of 'the popular', and of storytelling generally.

How IR theory makes sense of the world

Up to this point, we have analysed how IR theory makes sense of the world by asking questions about the stories told through individual IR myths. But what if we take our questions about sense-making and storytelling and apply them to IR theory as a whole? Then we will get an idea of how our individual IR myths work together – not only as a set of individual stories about international politics but as a general framework for storytelling.

To do this, let's return to those two questions that have guided us through our individual myths and recast them for IR theory generally:

1   How does IR theory make sense of the world?
2   What does IR theory say is typical and deviant in that world?

Mainstream IR theory (represented by realism, idealism, and Wendtian constructivism) makes sense of the world by focusing on specific actors, contexts, and interactions. As our first three myths tell us, the actors that matter in international politics are sovereign nation-states. According to realist, idealist, and constructivist myths, sovereign nation-states may just exist (as they seem to for realists and idealists) or their identities and interests may be the effects of practices (as constructivists claim). But in mainstream IR theory, both claims amount to the same thing. States are the fundamental actors in international politics, and all analysis of important events must begin and end with states.

The context in which states interact for mainstream IR theorists is not 'international politics' broadly defined but the tightly theorized realm of international anarchy. All mainstream IR theorists agree on the importance of international anarchy for understanding international politics. Debates and disagreements about the nature of anarchy (what it is 'really' like) and the effects of anarchy (what it makes states do) only serve to underscore the importance which mainstream IR theorists attach to it.

Finally, mainstream IR theorists concern themselves with sovereign nation-states in a situation of international anarchy because they are worried about a specific set of international interactions. These international interactions are found in what is often called the world of 'high politics', a world that focuses on diplomatic practices, on wars among sovereign nation-states, and increasingly on international economic issues like globalization. Other international interactions pale in comparison to the 'serious' questions of war and peace and the 'serious' activities undertaken by statespeople to confront and possibly resolve these issues (see Table 7.1).

One would be hard-pressed to find an IR theorist who does not take seriously questions of war and peace or of conflict more generally. Even so, many IR theorists contest the terms in which these questions are asked. One of the reasons for this is because, as mainstream IR theorists tell their stories about international politics and construct a template through which all 'serious' stories about IR theory must be told (must focus on states, anarchy, and diplomatic practice), they are (as we have seen in our individual IR myths) proscribing what is typical and deviant in the world of international politics and in the culture of IR theory. While mainstream IR theorists are happy to discuss what is typical and deviant in their world of international politics, they are less comfortable with interrogating the mainstream (dominant) culture of IR theory.

So, for example, following from how IR theorists make sense of the world (through states, anarchy, and diplomatic practice), IR theorists come up with some compelling 'truths' about the world of international politics. What is typical and deviant in this world in some ways depends upon which tradition of IR theory one subscribes to (realism, idealism, constructivism). For realists, the harsh realities of international life mean we will never overcome conflict among sovereign nation-states because we will never escape international anarchy (Chapter 2). For idealists, we might escape conflict either by moving out of international anarchy into an international hierarchy led by a world government, or we may escape conflict by mitigating state behaviour through an international society (Chapter 3). For constructivists, international outcomes are unclear. They will be conflictual (as realists claim) or cooperative (as idealists claim) depending upon what states make of anarchy (Chapter 4).

Yet while mainstream IR theorists cannot agree on what is typical and deviant within their general framework of states, anarchy, and diplomatic practice, critics of mainstream IR theory have no trouble showing what in their general theoretical framework for analysis is typical and deviant in IR theory. Not only does mainstream IR theory unduly confine analysis of international politics to questions about states,

Table 7.1 How does IR theory make sense of the world?

Actors	Sovereign nation-states
Context	International anarchy
Interactions	Practices of states and statespeople to confront and possibly resolve questions of war and peace

anarchy, and diplomatic/policy practices. In so doing, it is also typically ethnocentric, racist, classist, and sexist.

The North American centrism of IR theory begins with the nationalities of these authors, all of whom are North American, and this tells us something about which authors matter in the discipline of international relations (they are also all male, middle- or upper-class, and all but one is white). But, of course, an author's own subject position does not doom him or her to write from that position alone. Yet we find ethnocentric and other biases reproduced in our individual IR myths. Kegley's myth 'there is an international society' is among the best examples of ethnocentrism, for in this myth Kegley seems to mistake post-Cold War US hegemony for an international society (Chapter 3). Fukuyama's myth is another example. The liberalism that he so staunchly defends and supports the spread of globally is an Anglo-American-centric ideology, the power politics of which is never discussed (Chapter 6).

Race is another concept that seems to drop out of traditional IR theory. It seems to be assumed that the world of IR theory and international politics, like the world of most of the authors of our IR myths, is a white world. And white is taken as a non-race, as beyond race (Dyer, 1997). This may explain why none of our myths, bar one, explicitly addresses race. It is our one non-white theorist, Francis Fukuyama, who brings race into play in his theory, but he does so in a way that preserves the centrality of white cultures at the expense of non-white ones (Ling, 2000).

Class is another of those concepts that sits uncomfortably in relation to mainstream IR theory. This is not surprising for two reasons. First, all of our authors are North American (and all but one is US), and, second, class has never been a concept that has been terribly well interrogated in the US. Most US citizens of whatever economic or social group would call themselves 'middle-class'. Because of this, class often drops out of everyday and academic analyses. It is no exception in our mainstream IR myths. Nowhere is there any consideration of either economic or social classes (or even categories) within states, nor is there an analysis of classes *of* states (see Wallerstein, 1974, 1980, 1989). Worse still, myths like Fukuyama's 'it is the end of history' with its positive spin on globalization obscure class relations within and among sovereign nation-states, making any analysis of them all the more difficult (Chapter 6). If class is not considered in IR theory, then analysis of the power relations that keep some people, groups, and states 'upper-class' in international politics (like being 'great powers' or a hegemon) and other states in the 'lower class' of international politics (like 'third world' or 'postcolonial' states) will not find its way into core IR myths.

Finally, mainstream IR theory is gendered, and its gender is primarily masculine. Jones's lament aside (Chapter 5), IR theory has traditionally taken masculinely-engendered bodies and activities to be its objects of analysis, whether those gendered bodies/activities are (borrowing the title from Waltz's book) men, states, or war. Whether looking to realism or idealism, the theories of 'human' nature that IR theorists draw upon as building blocks of their theories about individuals, states, and their interactions are theories about the 'nature' of man (Chapter 2). As a result, not only individuals are gendered in IR theory. So too do we find 'gendered states' (Peterson, ed., 1992) and gendered activities like war (masculine) and peace (feminine) (Elshtain, 1987). And, as a reading of Jones's myth through *Fatal*

Table 7.2 What is typical and deviant for IR theory?

Typical	Deviant
• North American centric • racist • classist • masculinist	To defy or question the terms in which IR theory tells stories about international politics

Attraction highlights, when relationships among gendered bodies are considered by mainstream IR theorists, they seem to be exclusively heterosexual (Weber, 1999).

Taken together, mainstream IR theory makes sense of the world by focusing on states, anarchy, and diplomatic practice in ways that draw upon a particularly biased thinking about place, race, class, and sex. All of this is typical of mainstream IR theory. And if this is what is typical of mainstream IR theory, then it is easy to see how theories of international politics that defy and/or question the terms in which IR theory tells its stories about the world are labelled deviant. How Jones does this to feminist IR theory is the most elaborated example in this text (Chapter 5). Other examples are how constructivism constructs poststructuralism as deviant (Chapter 4) and how liberal theories of globalization construct historical materialism as deviant (Chapter 6).

This is not to suggest that feminism, poststructuralism, and historical materialism are free of any bias. These alternative perspectives on international politics depend upon their own mythologized understandings of the world, and their myths often employ the same or similar types of exclusions that mainstream IR theory does. The point, however, is that these alternative perspectives make some of the same 'mistakes' as traditional IR theory in different ways – ways which challenge the postulates for storytelling found in mainstream IR theory. It is for this reason – and not because they are themselves 'true stories' – that these alternative takes on international politics are 'deviant' from the perspective of traditional IR theory.

Making sense of IR theory

If this is how IR theory makes sense of the world – both the world of international politics and the world of IR theory, then how do we make sense of IR theory? What does all of this tell us about how IR theory relates to culture, ideology, mythology, and popular media like film? And, most crucially, where is the politics in all of this?

The argument put forward in this book is that IR theory is a site of cultural practice. It is a place where stories that make sense of our world are spun, where signifying practices about international politics take place, where meanings about international life are produced, reproduced, and exchanged. We have seen all of this illustrated in our five IR myths. Each of them makes sense of the world by telling a particular story about international politics. When we read these myths together (as we did in the last section), we find that IR theory is a site of cultural practice not only because it provides us with 'an ensemble of stories' we tell about international politics (Geertz, 1975:448). More importantly, *IR theory is a site of cultural practice because it provides a framework for storytelling itself.* Culturally, IR theory tells us not only what makes sense about the world of international politics out there, but it also tells us which stories in the realm of international theory we should take seriously in classrooms and at conferences and in policy meetings.

What this means is that how IR theory makes sense of the world through the stories it tells about international politics (either via specific myths like 'international anarchy is the permissive cause of war' or through broader traditions like realism) is already indebted to the template for storytelling that these IR myths and IR theories depend upon in order to appear to be meaningful, serious, and important. This has unsettling implications for mainstream IR theory. For what it means is that we cannot understand international politics by adopting an IR tradition as our guide or by memorizing IR's sacred myths. This is because IR traditions and myths are both products of and productive of IR theory as a cultural site where the 'giving and taking of meaning' (Hall, ed., 1997:2) about international politics and about IR theory itself occurs. In other words, IR theory as a model for storytelling has already restricted what international politics can mean as it is narrated by IR traditions and IR myths.

When we investigate IR theory as a site of culture, we find ideological practices at work. Reading our IR myths together as we did in the last section, we quickly spotted several named ideologies at work – ethnocentrism, racism, classism, and (hetero)sexism. These are the sorts of ideologies we have long been trained to look for. But another purpose of this text has been to demonstrate how ideologies work in less familiar ways that are more difficult to identify. They work, for example, through not only what we can name and say (conscious ideologies) but also through what we cannot name and what goes without saying (unconscious ideologies; Barthes, 1972:11). And, arguably, it is unconscious ideologies that are the most powerful. Since they are so difficult to identify, they are all the more difficult to examine critically.

When they crop up in IR theory, I call these unconscious or unnamed ideologies IR myths. They are *apparent truths*, usually expressed as a slogan, that an IR theory or tradition relies upon in order to appear to be true. They seem to be so true, so right on, so correct about the world of international politics that, to those adhering to the tradition that employs them, IR myths describe just the way things are. For a realist, international anarchy *is* the permissive cause of war. For an idealist, there *is* an international society. For a Wendtian constructivist, anarchy *is* what states make of it. And so on. But, as I have tried to point out, international politics is a lot more complicated than this. So how do IR traditions still get away with relying upon so many ideological positions as if they were not ideological positions but factually described the world as it is? They get away with it because, as I have suggested, these ideological positions are mythologized. They are transformed from what is seen to be 'cultural' and constructed into what is taken to be natural and therefore goes without saying. IR myths become habitual ways of thinking about the world of international politics.

We traced how the myth function in IR theory works by examining our individual IR myths. Ideologies are mythologized in IR theory by making sure what must go without saying in order for a myth to appear to be true is either deferred or displaced. Deferral means that the knowledge about the myth as a myth is delayed so much that we never receive it. Displacement means that the knowledge about a myth as a myth is placed beyond the bounds of our consideration. Some myths defer knowledge (we must never know that liberalism's empty core contradicts our desire for the good life or that fear is what makes us believe in either international anarchy as the permissive cause of war or international society as what will unify us in cooperation). Other myths work through displacement ('authors' must be placed behind productive practices so that they appear to be the producers of these practices, and gender must be placed within a variable so that feminist concerns can be placed outside the bounds of the discipline of IR). And, more often than not, deferral and displacement work together, even if one of them dominates.

This is what we see happening in the individual stories we read about IR theory. But what about IR theory as a whole? Is there a myth function to IR theory itself, greater than the sum of its individual IR myths? And, if so, how does it work? What does it defer or displace?

Just as individual IR myths tend to work at the level of stories, IR theory more generally works at the level of framing those stories. As a site of cultural practices, IR theory provides not just the stories about international politics but the framework which makes these stories meaningful, serious, and important. And it is this grid, this support, this basis for storytelling that goes without saying in IR theory itself – that it is reasonable, rational, and objective to narrate stories about IR theory which focus almost exclusively on sovereign nation-states in anarchy and the 'high political' practices their interactions give rise to. This is the 'Truth' of IR theory that makes other IR 'truths' possible. And, like any truth, this one may not be as true as it *appears* to be. For, as we have already seen, this premise for storytelling is indebted to numerous ideological positions, some of which are named and others of which are more difficult to name. So, somewhere along the line, *IR theory itself underwent (and is always really undergoing) a mythologizing function so that its framework for analysis appears to be natural, neutral, and common sense rather than cultural, ideological, and in need of critical analysis.*

What does this mean, then, that IR theory itself defers or displaces? Simple. It defers and displaces any knowledge that its stories and most importantly its framework for telling stories is mythologized. *IR theory defers and displaces the myth function itself.* How does it do this? *IR theory does this by placing critical examinations of IR theory beyond the bounds of meaningful, serious, and important IR theory.* This should not surprise us. For indeed, if IR theory did not do this, it could not function. Its myth function – both in terms of the specific stories it tells and in terms of its template for telling these stories – might be exposed. While exposing the myth function in IR theory would not put an end to it (for we never escape culture and

Table 7.3 IR theory's myth function

What IR theory defers	How IR theory defers it
The myth function itself	By (dis)placing criticism of IR theory beyond IR theory. Critique of IR theory does not count as serious IR theory itself

ideology), it may temporarily disrupt it. And if IR theory's myth function is disrupted, then this might open up new possibilities for uncharted stories about international politics to be told. This would be a terrible threat to traditional IR theory.

The politics of the popular

If exploring the myth function in IR theory is such a serious undertaking, then why have I carried it out by reading IR theory through a medium that lacks the status of serious – popular film? Hopefully, reading IR theory through popular film is more interesting and entertaining than it otherwise would be. And, for some, that might be reason enough for using films. But there are more important and indeed terribly serious reasons for using popular films (or other popular media that tell stories).

One reason for rethinking IR theory through popular film is that films bring the story aspects of IR theory into relief. We are accustomed to viewing films as narratives about specific worlds. We are less accustomed to viewing IR theory in this way. But, by pairing IR traditions and IR myths with a popular film, the drama, story points, flow, links, lapses, and effects of action are all easier to see.

Another reason for pairing IR theories with popular films is because popular films present all this drama and trauma to us in contained spatial and temporal locations. They offer up worlds that are familiar enough for us to relate to (like 1980s New York City in *Fatal Attraction* or 1990s Hollywood in *Wag the Dog*) without actually being those places. This is another reason why we can relate to popular films and relate them back to IR theory.

So, selecting popular films as a medium through which to revisit IR theory makes sense in part because popular films enable us to access what IR theory says, how it plots its story, and how all this together gives us a particular vision of the world. In effect, then, using popular film to help us think about IR theory seems to work because of some of the similarities between how films tell stories and how IR theory tells stories.

But even when we read IR theory through popular film, we assume that the kinds of stories told by IR theory and those told by popular film differ in important ways. The stories IR theory tells are supposedly 'true' stories. In contrast, popular films offer us stories that we know to be fictional. This is why the stories told in IR theory are taken seriously, whereas those in popular film are so often regarded as frivolous. We assume that popular films offer us escapes from reality, whereas IR theory confronts us with the hard facts about the world. And so, like mainstream IR theorists, we generally place IR theory in the realm of 'high culture' and 'high politics' while we place popular film in the realm of 'low culture' and 'low politics'. It might be fun to see how the realities of international life might be dramatized in popular films, but, as mainstream IR theorists warn us, we should guard against taking these dramatizations too seriously. They are not part of the 'cut and thrust' of international politics or of IR theory.

Or are they?

Each of the IR myths we have looked at is paired with a popular film. In some cases this is because the film plays out the plot of an IR theory (as in the cases of *Lord of the Flies* and *Independence Day*). But while parallel plots might be one reason for the pairing of films and myths in some cases, *in every case films and myths are paired because they produce and circulate the same myth*. The myth we find about anarchy in Waltz's books *Man, the State, and War* and *Theory of International Politics* is the same myth we find in the film *Lord of the Flies*. The myth we find about the author function in Wendt's essay 'Anarchy is What States make of It' is the same myth we find in the film *Wag the Dog*. The myth we find in Fukuyama's essay 'The End of History?' is the same myth we find in the film *The Truman Show*. And on and on.

If the same myths we find in serious IR theory are also at play in shallow popular films, then what does this mean for each of these mythologized sites and the relationship between them? Are films more serious then we at first thought? Is IR theory more trivial than we dared to imagine? Does this pairing of the 'popular' and the 'serious' transform them both? If so, where do we now locate 'high culture' and 'high politics' and 'low culture' and 'low politics'?

Pairing 'serious' IR theory with 'superficial' popular films suggests that IR theory may not be located in the realm of 'truth' and 'reality' any more than popular films are. Maybe IR theory is just a bunch of stories that, like popular films, mixes and mythologizes fact and fiction. And since the stories and myths we find in IR theory are often the same ones we find in popular films, then this pairing of IR theory and film shows that the meanings IR theory uses to make sense of the world are not only produced and circulated in traditional academic 'high cultural' realms but in popular 'low cultural' locations as well. If the work of propagating and circulating IR myths occurs in popular films as well as in IR theories, then neglecting this realm of 'low politics' in our attempts to come to grips with how the world works would be a mistake. We must interrogate IR theory as a site of cultural practice *wherever* it occurs – in classic IR texts, in classrooms, and in more popular sites of culture like film, literature, art, and television.

Maybe popular films do a lot more political work than we at first credited them with doing. Not only do they illustrate (and sometimes overtly critique) the stories found in IR myths by circulating similar (or different) myths. Popular films tell us 'too much' about IR theory. They also tell us how IR myths function. They do this by showing us what must go without saying in order for a myth to appear to be true. And, most importantly, *popular films dramatize for us how what must go without saying is*

Box 7.1 Why pair IR theory with popular films?

1 Films bring IR theory's story points into relief
2 Films offer us contained, nearly parallel worlds in which to critically rethink IR theory
3 IR myths and popular films produce and circulate similar myths. Therefore, we must analyse the popular in order to understand IR myths and international politics
4 Pairing popular films with serious IR theory exposes IR theory as a mythologized mix of fact and fiction
5 Popular films dramatize the myth function of IR theory and how what must go without saying is deferred and displaced

kept in the place of non-knowledge through strategies of deferral and displacement. That's a lot of work for a frivolous medium to do!

But if popular films do a lot of serious political work by de-mythologizing and re-politicizing IR myths (Barthes, 1972), then why are investigations of popular films so often relegated to the netherlands of the negligible by IR theorists – to 'mere' cultural studies or film theory which they take to be superficial and therefore unimportant? One answer might be that IR theorists simply do not yet appreciate how the popular functions politically in relation to international politics and inter-national theory. Because they don't appreciate it, they don't take it seriously. For this reason, these sorts of IR theorists simply ignore popular cultural phenomena.

A more cynical answer might be that IR theorists do recognize how the popular functions politically in relation to international politics and international theory. They sense how the popular might function resistively and disruptively in relation to cherished IR traditions and the IR myths that make them appear to be true. And they recognize that taking the popular seriously might challenge the very framework through which IR theory tells its stories about international politics. For this reason, these sorts of IR theorists might work to defer a widespread appreciation of what the popular might do to IR theory, and they might work to replace the popular in the realm of the frivolous before the popular displaces IR theory from the realm of the serious.

And, of course, there is a third reason why IR theorists might not take the political power of the popular seriously. They might be so taken in by their own mythologized ways of viewing the relationship between the political and the popular that they can no longer imagine this relationship differently. This is why, for these theorists, the popular belongs in a different realm from the political.

Whether by neglect, by design, or by displacement, the politics of the popular is among the most undervalued and therefore underanalysed aspects of international politics. And this is a grave oversight for both mainstream and critical IR theorists. For the popular poses a significant challenge to IR's cherished cultural practices.

Where does all of this leave us?

So, where does all of this leave us? Hopefully, it leaves us knowing 'too much' about IR theory and IR myths – not because of what they say but because of what they do culturally *and* politically. Indeed, thinking about IR theory as a site of cultural practice through formal, academic cultural practices like writing IR theories and myths and through less formal cultural practices like popular films has demonstrated that *all cultural sites are powerful arenas in which political struggles take place.* And, maybe most importantly, this way of rethinking IR theory has helped us to rethink the relationship between culture and politics. *Culture is not opposed to politics. Culture is political, and politics is cultural.*

What this means is that the cultural stories all of us tell – whether in film, in IR theory, or in everyday life – are political. Knowing how stories function – what makes them appear to be true – gives us the means to both critique and create politically powerful stories.

Bibilography

Althusser, Louis (1969) *For Marx*. London: Allen Lane.

Ashley, Richard K. (1984) 'The Poverty of Neorealism', *International Organization* 38(2):225–86.

—— (1989) 'Living on Borderlines: Man, Poststructuralism, and War', in James Der Derian and Michael Shapiro (eds) *International/Intertextual Relations: Postmodern Readings of World Politics*. Lexington, Mass.: Lexington Books.

Ball, Terrance and Richard Dagger (1995) *Political Ideologies and the Democratic Ideal*, 2nd edition. New York: Harper Collins.

Barthes, Roland (1972) *Mythologies*, trans. Annette Lavers. New York: Noonday Press.

—— (1974) *S/Z: An Essay*, trans. Richard Miller. New York: Hill and Wang.

Baudrillard, Jean (1987) *Seduction*, trans. Brian Singer. New York: St. Martin's Press.

Baylis, John and Steve Smith (eds) (1997) *The Globalization of World Politics*. Oxford: Oxford University Press.

Biersteker, Thomas and Cynthia Weber (eds) (1996) *State Sovereignty as Social Construct*. Cambridge: Cambridge University Press.

Bleiker, Roland (1997) 'Forget IR Theory', *Alternatives* 22(1):57–85.

Bull, Hedley (1987) *The Anarchical Society*. London: Macmillian.

Buzan, Barry, Charles Jones, and Richard Little (1993) *The Logic of Anarchy: Neorealism to Structural Realism*. New York: Columbia University Press.

Campbell, David (1992) *Writing Security*. Minneapolis: University of Minnestoa Press.

Carroll, Berenice (1972) 'Peace Research: The Cult of Power', *Journal of Conflict Resolution* 16(4):585–616.

Carver, Terrell (1996) *Gender is Not a Synonym for Women*. Boulder, Col.: Lynne Rienner.

Carver, Terrell, Molly Cochran, and Judith Squires (1998) 'Gendering Jones: Feminisms, IRs, Masculinities', *Review of International Studies* 24(2):283–97.

Conlon, James (1996) 'The Place of Passion: Reflections on *Fatal Attraction*', in Barry Keith Grant (ed.) *The Dread of Difference: Gender and the Horror Film*. Austin: University of Texas Press, pp. 401–11.

Connell, Robert W. (1995) *Masculinities*. Cambridge: Cambridge University Press.

Debrix, François (1999) *Reinvisioning Peacekeeping: The United Nations and the Mobilization of Ideology*. Minneapolis: University of Minnesota Press.

135

De Certeau, Michel (1988) *The Practice of Everyday Life*, trans. Steven F. Rendall. Berkeley: University of California Press.

Doty, Roxanne Lynn (1996) *Imperial Encounters: The Politics of Representation in North–South Relations*. Minneapolis: University of Minnesota Press.

Dyer, Richard (1985) 'Taking Popular Television Seriously', in David Lusted and Phillip Drummond (eds) *TV and Schooling*. London: British Film Institute, pp. 41–6.

—— (1997) *White*. London: Routledge.

Edkins, Jenny (1999) *Poststructuralism and International Relations: Bringing the Political Back In*. Boulder, Col.: Lynne Rienner.

Elshtain, Jean Bethke (1987) *Women and War*. New York: Basic Books.

Enloe, Cynthia (1989) *Bananas, Beaches and Bases: Making Feminist Sense of International Politics*. Berkeley: University of California Press.

Ermarth, Elizabeth Deeds (1992) *Sequel to History: Postmodernism and the Crisis of Representational Time*. Princeton: Princeton University Press.

Foucault, Michel (1980) *Power/Knowledge*, trans. C. Gordon, L. Marshall, J. Mepham, and K. Soper. Hemel Hampstead: Harvester Wheatsheaf.

—— (1984) 'What is an Author?', in Paul Rabinow (ed.) *The Foucault Reader*. New York: Pantheon, pp. 101–20.

Fukuyama, Francis (1989) 'The End of History?' *The National Interest* 16 (Summer):2–18.

—— (1992) *The End of History and the Last Man*. London: Hamish Hamilton.

Geertz, Clifford (1975) *The Interpretation of Cultures*. London: Hutchinson.

George, Jim (1994) *Discourses of Global Politics: A Critical (Re)introduction to International Relations*. Boulder, Col.: Lynne Rienner.

Gilpin, Robert (1983) *War and Change in World Politics*. Cambridge: Cambridge University Press.

Grant, Rebecca and Kathleen Newland (eds) (1991) *Gender and International Relations*. Milton Keynes: Open University Press.

Hall, Stuart (ed.) (1997) *Representations: Cultural Representations and Signifying Practices*. Milton Keynes: Open University Press.

Hay, Colin and David Marsh (eds) (2000) *Demystifying Globalization*. Boulder, Col.: St. Martin's Press.

Herod, Andrew, Gearóid Ó Tuathail, and Susan M. Roberts (eds) (1998) *An Unruly World? Globalization, Governance, and Geography*. London: Routledge.

Hirst, Paul and Grahame Thompson (1996) *Globalization in Question*. Cambridge: Polity Press.

Huntington, Samuel P. (1993) 'The Clash of Civilizations?', *Foreign Affairs* 72 (Summer): 22–49.

Jackson, Robert (1990) *Quasi-States: Sovereignty, International Relations and the Third World*. Cambridge: Cambridge University Press.

Jameson, Fredric and Masao Miyoshi (eds) (1998) *The Cultures of Globalization*. Chapel Hill, N.C.: Duke University Press.

Jones, Adam (1996) 'Does "Gender" make the World go Round? Feminist Critiques of International Relations', *Review of International Studies* 22(4):405–29.

—— (1998) 'Engendering Debate', *Review of International Studies* 24(2):299–303.

Kegley, Charles W., Jr. (1993) 'The Neoidealist Moment in International Studies? Realist Myths and the New Internatonal Realities', *International Studies Quarterly* 37 (June):131–46.

—— (ed.) (1995) 'The Neoliberal Challenge to Realist Theories of World Politics: An introduction', in Charles W. Kegley, Jr., *Controversies in International Relations Theory: Realism and the Neoliberal Challenge*. New York: St. Martin's Press, pp. 1–24.

Keohane, Robert O. (1984) *After Hegemony*. Princeton: Princeton University Press.

—— (ed.) (1986) *Neorealism and its Critics*. New York: Columbia University Press.

—— (1988) 'International Institutions: Two Approaches', *International Studies Quarterly* 32:379–96.

—— (1989) 'International Relations Theory: Contributions of a Feminist Standpoint', *Millennium* 18(2):245–53.

Kofman, Eleonore and Gillian Youngs (eds) (1996) *Globalization: Theory and Practice*. London: Pinter.

Krasner, Stephen D. (ed.) (1983) *International Regimes*. Ithaca: Cornell University Press.

Kublakova, V., Nicholas Greenwood Onuf, and Paul Kowert (eds) (1998) *International Relations in a Constructed World*. New York: M.E. Sharpe.

Lapid, Yosef and Freidrich Kratochwil (eds) (1996) *The Return of Culture and Identity in IR Theory*. Boulder, Col.: Lynne Rienner.

Leyshon, Andrew (1997) 'True Stories?: Global Dreams, Global Nightmares, and Writing Globalization', in Rodger Lee and Jane Wills (eds) *Geographies of Economies*. London: Arnold Press, pp. 133–46.

Ling, Lily (2000) 'Hypermasculinity on the Rise, Again: A Response to Fukuyama on Women and World Politics', *International Feminist Journal of Politics* 2(2):277–86.

MacKinnon, Catherine (1989) *Toward a Feminist Theory of the State*. Cambridge, Mass., Harvard University Press.

Marchand, Marianne (2000) 'Gendered Representations of the "Global": Reading/Writing Globalization', in Richard Stubbs and Geoffrey R.D. Underhill (eds) *Political Economy and the Changing Global Order*, 2nd edition. Oxford: Oxford University Press, pp. 218–28.

Micklethwait, John and Adrian Wooldridge (2000) *The Future Perfect: The Challenges and Hidden Promises of Globalization*. New York: Times Press.

Mirzoeff, Nicholas (1999) *Visual Culture*. London: Routledge.

Modelski, George (1987) *Long Cycles in World Politics*. Seattle: University of Washington Press.

Monaco, James (2000) *How to Read a Film*. Oxford: Oxford University Press.

Murphy, Craig (1996) 'Seeing Women, Recognizing Gender, Recasting International Relations', *International Organization* 50(3):513–38.

Onuf, Nicholas Greenwood (1989) *World of our Making*. Columbia: University of South Carolina Press.

—— (1999) 'Worlds of our Making: The Strange Career of Constructivism in IR', in Donald J. Puchala (ed.) *Visions of IR*. Columbia: University of South Carolina Press.

O'Sullivan, Tim, et al. (1994) *Key Concepts in Communication and Cultural Studies*. London: Routledge.

Ó Tuathail, G. (1998) 'Political Geography III: Dealing with Deterritorialization?', *Progress in Human Geography* 22:81–93.

Peterson, V. Spike (ed.) (1992) *Gendered States: Feminist (Re)Visions of International Relations Theory*. Boulder, Col.: Lynne Rienner.

Pettman, Ralph (1998) 'Sex, Power, and the Grail of Positive Collaboration', in Marysia Zalewski and Jane Parpart, (eds) *The 'Man' Question in International Relations*. Boulder, Col.: Westview, pp. 169–84.

Rogin, Michael (1998) *Independence Day*. London: British Film Institute.

Ruddick, Sara (1990) *Maternal Thinking: Toward a Politics of Peace*. London: The Women's Press.

Ruggie, John G. (1998) *Constructing the World Polity*. London: Routledge.

Said, Edward (1978) *Orientalism: Western Conceptions of the Orient*. London: Penguin.

Saper, Craig J. (1997) *Artificial Mythologies: A Guide to Cultural Intervention*. Minneapolis: University of Minnesota Press.

Storey, John (1997) *An Introduction to Cultural Theory and Popular Culture*, 2nd edition, London: Prentice Hall.

Strange, Susan (1996) *The Retreat of the State*. Cambridge: Cambridge University Press.

Sylvester, Christine (1994) *Feminist Theory and International Relations in a Postmodern Era*. Cambridge: Cambridge University Press.

Tickner, J. Ann (1992) *Gender in International Relations: Feminist Perspectives on Achieving Global Security*. New York: Columbia University Press.

Walker, R.B.J. (1993) *Inside/Outside: International Relations as Political Theory*. Cambridge: Cambridge University Press.

Wallerstein, Immanuel (1974, 1980, 1989) *The Modern World-System*, 3 vols, San Diego: Academic Press.

Walt, Stephen M. (1998) 'International Relations: One world, Many theories', *Foreign Policy* (Spring):29–46.

Waltz, Kenneth (1959) *Man, the State, and War*. New York: Columbia University Press.

—— (1979) *Theory of International Politics*. Reading, Mass.: Addison-Wesley.

Webber, Julie (1998) 'Independence Day as a Cosmopolitan Moment: Teaching International Relations' (unpublished paper).

Weber, Cynthia (1994) 'Good Girls, Little Girls, and Bad Girls: Male Paranoia in Robert Keohane's Critique of Feminist International Relations', *Millennium* 23(2):337–49.

—— (1998) 'Reading Martin Wight's "Why is There No International Theory?" as History', *Alternatives* 23:451–69.

—— (1999) *Faking It: US hegemony in a 'Post-Phallic' Era*. Minneapolis: University of Minnestoa Press.

Wendt, Alexander (1992) 'Anarchy is What States make of It: The Social Construction of Power Politics', *International Organization* 46:391–425. Reprinted in James Der Derian (ed.) (1995) *International Theory: Critical Investigations*. New York: New York University Press, pp. 129–77.

—— (1994) 'Collective Identity Formation and the International State', *American Political Science Review* 88(2):384–96.

—— (1999) *Social Theory of International Politics*. Cambridge: Cambridge University Press.

Weldes, Jutta (1999) 'Going Cultural: *Star Trek*, State Action, and Popular Culture', *Millennium* 28(1):117–34.

Williams, Raymond (1983) *Keywords*. London: Fontana.

Zalewski, Marysia (1993) 'Feminist Standpoint Theory meets International Relations Theory', *Fletcher Forum* (Summer):13–32.

—— (1995) 'Well, What is the Feminist Perspective on Bosnia?', *International Affairs* 71(2):339–56.

—— (1999) 'Where is Woman in International Relations?: "To return as a woman and be heard"', *Millennium* 27:847–67.

—— and Jane Parpart (eds) (1998) *The 'Man' Question in International Relations*. Boulder, Col.: Westview.

Index